DARING
FAITH

Also available
A 12-WEEK COMPANION DVD SERIES
Get your copy today.
www.leafwoodpublishers.com

RANDY HARRIS
GREG TAYLOR

DARING
FAITH

Meeting Jesus in
the Book of John

LEAFWOOD
PUBLISHERS
an imprint of Abilene Christian University Press

DARING FAITH
Meeting Jesus in the Book of John

L E A F W O O D
P U B L I S H E R S
an imprint of Abilene Christian University Press

Copyright © 2016 by Randy Harris and Greg Taylor

ISBN 978-0-89112-346-0

Printed in the United States of America

Cover design by Rachel Mallary
Interior text design by Sandy Armstrong, Strong Design

Leafwood Publishers is an imprint of Abilene Christian University Press

ACU Box 29138
Abilene, Texas 79699
1-877-816-4455
www.leafwoodpublishers.com

18 19 20 21 / 7 6 5 4 3 2

For our dads
Cecil Harris and Terrel Taylor

ACKNOWLEDGMENTS

God's love compels us to speak and write, so we first thank our Father, the Son, and the Holy Spirit.

Second, we thank the churches we serve in for listening to us and helping us shape our preaching and teaching.

Third, we thank our families and friends, who keep us laughing and full of joy.

Fourth, we thank our publisher and editors. Thank you to Duane Anderson, Phil Dosa, Mary Hardegree, Lettie Morrow, Seth Shaver, Jason Fikes, Rachel Mallary, and Gene Shelburne. Each had a role in inspiring the book, giving it a title, conceiving the cover, and producing the video and book together as a useful resource for churches, groups, families, and individuals. With a strong editorial hand, Gene Shelburne read and copyedited the manuscript, wrangling a stray calf here, power sanding down rough edges there, and smoothing out what you now find as a readable text.

Fifth, thank you to Harding School of Theology Library that provided books for research on the Gospel of John when we needed them, and thanks to New Life Ranch, a valley set apart for Christ near West Siloam, Arkansas, a good place to reflect and write.

Sixth, we thank scholars and preachers whose resources on John function in ways this resource cannot. Robert Kysar's *The Maverick Gospel* is indispensable for John study. Thanks also to David Fleer and Dave Bland for putting together a book of essays and sermons no one preaching on John ought to be without. John Barton was the first to show the differences in the four Gospel accounts in a way his college roommate and mission teammate, Greg, could truly grasp. You'll see an expanded version of this written out in the chapter called, "The Weirdest Gospel." Michael Card's book and companion CD on John inspired us to imagine more vividly, and we highly recommend his musical biblical storytelling. If we hadn't already dedicated the book to our dads, we could dedicate this book to a spiritual father of the study of John for people worldwide in this age: the late Raymond Brown. If you don't get everything you want out of our book, you'll likely get more than you want from Brown's works on John.

Finally, many thanks to you, dear reader, because your desire for daring faith inspires us as we write and speak.

TABLE OF CONTENTS

Introduction

*"I would like to acknowledge my four writers,
Matthew, Mark, Luke, and John."*
—Bishop Fulton J. Steen (1895–1979)

THE PURPOSE OF THIS BOOK IS TO INSPIRE YOU TO daring faith by meeting Jesus in the book of John.

We do this by entering into stories and teachings of Jesus, as well as events of his crucifixion and resurrection, then issuing you a series of dares. We recommend you read the book and watch the companion videos with others, including those who believe, those who doubt, and those who do not believe in Jesus.

In the book you will find us writing in the plural "we," with a few exceptions such as sidebars that we sign with Randy or Greg. This is the second video and book we've produced together in which Randy talks and Greg writes. Our overall goal is to bring resources for Christian churches that help make disciples who grow deeper in love with Jesus and get serious about living his teachings.

A man walked into a library to return a book. The librarian asked if the book had been good. "Definitely not the best book I've ever read on the subject," said the man. "So, you've read a lot on the subject?" asked the librarian. "No, this book is the first."

Better books on the Gospel of John already exist. And this may be your first book to read on John. Still, we make no assumptions that this will be the best you've read on the subject. Our aim is to help inspire daring faith in Jesus. If we succeed in our aim, please pass the word along to friends, family, and enemies.

We believe this book is going to inspire you, but not like typical Christian inspirational books. We are teachers and preachers, so our book is not just a good read to motivate you to live your dreams. Instead, we're interested in all of us learning how to read the Bible to discover God's dreams for the world. So we want to see you increase your skills in reading the Bible with sound logic, imagination, joy, and obedience.

Yes, you can find more comprehensive books on John, and this is not a commentary or an exhaustive book that details every verse of John. If you want that, then get Raymond Brown's two-volume Anchor commentary on the Gospel of John. It's so exhaustive that it will also double as a booster chair for your three-year-old at the table. Raymond Brown died in 1998, but his monumental work has influenced nearly everyone who teaches on the Gospel of John. One of our favorite books by Brown is a more compact and humorous *A Retreat with John the Evangelist*.

We'd like this to be the most practical book you've ever read on the Gospel of John. So we are approaching John as we did the Sermon on the Mount in our previous book and DVD set, *Living Jesus.* The companion video, also titled *Daring Faith,* is a dozen short segments you can watch in a group, church, with your family, or alone with some popcorn. The chapters in the book match the segments of the video, but you will find extra content in the book.

Have you ever played the childhood game, Truth or Dare? With each story or teaching segment, we offer you a series of activities in the form of truths *and* dares. Similar to the game, we'll ask some questions to draw out truths from each of the chapters we cover in John and dare you to live them. We won't dare you to do anything we wouldn't do. We take the Bible and the teachings of Jesus seriously, but we try not to take ourselves too seriously. As cliché as that sounds, we challenge you to do the same: take the Bible seriously and yourself less seriously. The questions in the Truth and Dare section of each chapter come from the Discovery Bible Study method, a basic inductive Bible study method that emphasizes prayer, reading the text and asking good questions in community, obeying, and sharing with others what you've experienced. One good resource for Discovery Bible Study is Kevin King and http://nycinternationalproject.org/.

The best way to understand a book of the Bible is not to read our book. The best way to understand the Gospel of John is to read the Gospel of John. So, our introductory dare is for you to read the Gospel of John.

Many of us try to understand bits and pieces of the Bible, a teaching here, a sermon there, a book like this, and we often neglect to read the Bible texts well. We dare you to read the entire Gospel of John. First, skim all twenty-one chapters of John briskly, and do not get bogged down or distracted. Get a feel for the way the story is structured, the order, teachings, and action.

If this book does what it's supposed to do, you will read the Gospel of John more than our book, and we'll do our best to guide you in further readings of particular stories. These readings will help you enter the stories of men and women who meet Jesus in the book of John.

This book is about daring faith in the God who became one of us. The goal of this book will be fulfilled when you risk your life in daring faith in the person of Jesus Christ as he has been revealed in the Gospel of John.

INTRODUCTION DARE

Read or skim the main headings and stories of the Gospel of John.

1. What do you like about the book of John so far?
2. What do you not like about John?
3. What do you think the Gospel of John is saying to the audience that originally received it?
4. What is the Gospel of John saying to us today?
5. What is the Gospel of John calling us to believe?
6. What is the Gospel of John calling us to do?
7. With whom can you share this dare to read the Gospel of John this week?

TRUTH & DARE

DARE ONE:
The Weirdest Gospel

"John's Gospel is deep enough for an elephant to swim, but it's shallow enough for a child not to drown."
—Attributed to St. Augustine of Hippo

A ROBOTICS LAB IS AN AMAZING PLACE. PEOPLE work with robots, 3D printers, and drones. It's like being in a sci-fi movie. When we were in high school, we built birdhouses. Now high school students build robots. Entering John's world is like walking into a robotics lab, because it's so unique. John is building this magnificent picture of Jesus the Christ that is unlike any other we see.

John is by far the most unique of the four Gospels. About ninety percent of the content of the Gospel of John is not included in the other three Gospels. In parts, compared to the other three accounts of Jesus, the Gospel of John is just plain weird. If Matthew, Mark, and Luke are from different countries, then John is from another planet.

Matthew is like an intricate Jewish portrait. Matthew's account suits the teacher, covering various teachings of Jesus systematically. Stained glass in some churches depicts the four Gospels. Matthew is portrayed as a Lion, because the apostle wants us to know Jesus is the Messiah, what Jews called the Lion of Judah.

Luke suits the minister, with much sympathy for the poor. He portrays Jesus as a friend of sinners. The stained-glass image of Luke is an ox, because Jesus is pictured as a Suffering Servant. Luke is like a long-playing historical epic movie, with the Acts of the Apostles about the early church as its sequel.

Mark is like a play-by-play sportscast, full of action and headlines. The stained glass of Mark is a man, because the action is told in terse prose and is plain, like the man.

Mark's clear-cut account suits the missionary, while John's account is contemplative, not moving from action to action like Mark, but pausing at great lengths to delve more deeply into the teachings of Jesus and into what his life means and symbolizes.

John's Gospel is more like an x-ray, revealing the heart of Jesus and the relationship he has with his Father in heaven and the Holy Spirit who is given to live with believers forever. The x-ray examines the disciples' hearts, too, and we all are exposed for whether or not our faith truly has backbone. The stained glass of John's Gospel is an eagle, looking into the brilliance of the sun. Likewise, John's Gospel stares into the heart of God as Father, Son, and Holy Spirit, and does not shrink back from the brilliance of light and life that are revealed.

English Bible translations today are good enough that most people could read the Gospel of John without introduction, but because John's Gospel is so weird, we want to relay several things you ought to know before you read.

The first thing to keep in mind while you read is John's purpose. John is the only Gospel with a clearly stated purpose that seems aimed at helping unbelievers believe.

"But these are written that you may believe that Jesus is the Messiah, the Son of God, and that by believing you may have life in his name" (John 20:31).

Readers might assume that the "you" John addresses here is only unbelievers, but it's unlikely that John wrote for a general non-Christian audience. Most biblical writings were addressed to believing communities. We're convinced that John was written not simply to get unbelievers to believe but also to get *Christians* to continue believing. The Greek word used in 20:31 is *pisteuo*, which can be translated with the continuous present tense as "continue to believe." Of course, John wants unbelievers to believe, but his concern is primarily for those whose faith is in jeopardy in the community, starting where he had been living in Ephesus and expanding from there. John wants to give them reasons for daring faith even though they're starting to pay a price of persecution for their faith.

Second, keep in mind that while the other Gospels were written toward the middle of the first century, John wrote nearer to the end of that century, about 85 AD. Think about the date for a moment and how long it was after Jesus left the earth, about 30 AD. This time span between 30 and 85 AD makes the Gospel of John a second-generation document. John is the only Gospel written to people—like us—who never saw Jesus face to face or witnessed these events.

Imagine that we are Christians in the first century. We are Jews and a few Gentile converts who believe Jesus is the Messiah, but we've never met him face to face. We assemble in a synagogue, a place for religious worship and instruction. John is the last living eyewitness to the events of Jesus's life. His account is the mind and memory of a disciple inspired by the Holy Spirit to address the unbelief and creeping doubt of believers and unbelievers.

By the time John writes, it is becoming clear that Christians are something more than a branch of Judaism. People are being kicked out of the synagogue for believing Jesus is the Messiah. Opponents to Christianity know that the most effective means of keeping Christians from taking over their synagogues is to discredit their Founder. The most obvious thing to say in order to discredit Jesus is that he died a shameful death, executed by Romans. That's nothing like a Messiah. Why would you hitch your wagon to him? Why risk your life?

If you are still imagining you are a Christian in the first century, you are now wondering if believing in Jesus is worth it or not. Christians are starting to reconsider believing in Jesus, because if it's going to cost us friendships, a place in the synagogue, even our lives, then maybe we shouldn't be Jesus's followers at all.

The risk of believing in Jesus is utter loss of reputation. Getting put out of the synagogue is more than merely losing your pew at church. When someone today says, "He lost everything," they mean a person's family, job, and social standing. That's what it feels like to us in the first century to lose our place in the synagogue.

Let's assume this is the background of John, and we expect you'll see in your reading that many stories resonate with this basic background. What does it mean to be a follower of Jesus, whom you haven't seen, and why should you follow One who died the shameful death on the cross? As a result of this basic background and story, John comes across harshly toward a group he calls "the Jews." Most of the Christians were also Jews, but "the Jews" became John's shorthand for those who opposed the disciples and Jesus.

Because of this characterization of "the Jews," some have accused John of being anti-Semitic. Three brief points about this accusation. First, racism is antithetical to the gospel message. Second, "the Jews" represents an opponent group that serves in the story as a foil for the truth of the Messiah, but no violence is implied or called for against these opponents. Third, probably we should factor in the inescapable reality that John is himself a Jew. Would he write ugly comments about his own race?

Now back to our reflections on how to understand John's message. A third thing to remember as you read John is a point about grammar. We're going to do a little bit of Grammar 101 here, but please relax—it should be relatively painless. You'll feel a little stick while we deaden the pain, then we'll only run the drill for a few seconds.

Here goes: some English words have both a noun and verb form. Without this concept, you could not sing, "I dreamed a dream." Lots of English words are like this. We can dream a dream, hope a hope, iron with an iron. Not all English words, however, have a verb and noun form. For example, the noun *faith* has no corresponding verb form. Instead, what we say for the verb *faith* is, "I believe." What's important about this is that in Greek, the language John was written in, the noun and the verb form of *faith* are essentially the same. Faith, therefore, can be more than something you *have*. More accurately faith is something you *do*. The best way we can translate this into literal English is that we "faith Jesus."

What does this matter? In twenty-one chapters in John, the noun for *faith* does not appear, not once. Nowhere in John does he ever use the noun *faith*. The verb form, however, is everywhere. In English we read the verb as "believe." Get ready, because here's the whole point of this brief grammar "drilling." If *faith* had a verb form in English, "I believe" could also be translated as "I faith."

We're done with the grammar lesson, but here is the important thing to remember. In John, faith is not something you merely *have*. Faith is a verb. Faith is something you *do*. In John the crucial question is not, "Do you believe something is true?" The crucial question is, "When you are pressed and you may have to pay a price for it, will you *faith* Jesus or not?" We're going to see this over and over in John, in the stories he tells about people meeting Jesus. In John, faith is not something you *have*—it's something you *do*.

This book is a two-man campaign to give the word *faith* a verb form in English, but it's not going well. We couldn't convince our wise publishers to title the book *Faithing the Truth*, so we settled for the better title you now see on the cover.

The fourth thing to remember when you dare to read and live the Gospel of John is that Jesus does not teach the same way in John as he does in the other Gospels. For example, John contains no parables like the ones Jesus teaches in the other Gospels. None. John instead writes metaphors about Jesus, rather than parables about farming, shepherding, and finding coins, as in other Gospels. In John, Jesus uses metaphors such as "I am the bread of life," and hearers usually misunderstood.

Faithful reading of John's Gospel and "joining" the disciples and the crowd is to be ready to admit when we don't understand. Nodding or pretending that it means more to us than it really does serves no one. We must learn to ask good questions along with the disciples and those first hearers.

Michael Card points out in his excellent book and companion CD on the Gospel of John that instead of parable stories, Jesus is the living parable. "I am bread. I am living water. I am the good shepherd. I am the true vine." To better understand what John is doing, you have to pay attention to those different metaphors he uses. You have to pay attention to the fact that every metaphor serves one main purpose: to show us in terms we can understand who God-in-the-flesh really is.

The fifth thing to remember when you read is that John doesn't seem very interested in telling the story in strict chronological order. This bothers a lot of people and may bother you as you read, because John changes the common story order from the other Gospels. Before we get too upset with this, here's one way to think about this apparent lack of time order.

If we want to tell you about a trip we took, we may start from the first stagecoach or jet airplane out of town and tell it from start to every potty stop, till the boring finish. But if we want to make it interesting, we'll hit the high points, and sometimes we'll tell it out of order for a reason. If you wanted to tell us about your day, you could tell us about getting up, brushing your teeth, eating breakfast, drinking coffee (what kind and how much). You could tell us about your day in chronological order. Or, you could tell us about the people you met and a few highlights about what you did. It's also very likely you'll tell some things out of order. The chronological story would not be truer than the non-linear story. They are just different ways of arranging the content of your day.

Granted, there is much difference between recapping your day and telling the story of Jesus. But our point is that John clearly arranged the material in different ways from the synoptic Gospels. Matthew, Mark, and Luke are called "synoptic" partly because they are so similar in their arrangement of the details of the story of Jesus. John's arrangement is quite different, so he gets left out of the club. John is telling the story of Jesus to make particular points, but because he arranges it in a unique way doesn't make it untrue. It doesn't mean it didn't happen.

John's purpose is not like Luke's, to tell an orderly chronological account of Jesus and the life of the early church. As Clement of Alexandria put it, John wrote a "spiritual gospel," and since he did not seem as interested in the order of events, we're not going to concern ourselves too much with chronology either. It's important to note, however, that because of John's mention of three Passovers, some readers of John believe this confirms that Jesus's public ministry was three years long.

John has an order and content all his own. He had more time to reflect on the meaning of the events the synoptic Gospels report. John alone includes a prologue, much like a Greek play. Action in John centers more in Judea than in Galilee, as it does in the synoptics. John alone tells stories about people like Nicodemus and the Samaritan woman. Only John shows Jesus washing the disciples' feet, but he excludes the prayer in the Garden before the capture, and John doesn't mention the disciples falling asleep. On the other hand, Jesus's long prayer for the disciples and the world is found only in John.

Like Mark, John shows Jesus doing miracles, but he sandwiches them between long teachings by Jesus. John wants to arrange his story to get the maximum impact, but he doesn't write a movie script or play-by-play like the Gospel of Mark. For example, while every Gospel tells the story of the feeding of the multitudes, John alone includes a long metaphoric teaching about Jesus as the bread of life.

We recommend that you see a new attempt at making the Gospel of John watchable as a movie. Lots of creative editing and storytelling went into keeping the story moving, and it's well worth watching. Released in 2015 on Netflix, *The Gospel of John* was produced by the BBC, directed by David Batty, and smartly acted by Selva Rasalingam as Jesus.

The final thing to remember as you read is that John more than the synoptics emphasizes the divinity of Jesus, more than his humanity. As we go through the book, we'll be looking at some places where that's clearly true. And we'll get there by looking at a particular background of the Gospel that may have heightened John's need to focus on the divinity of Jesus.

If Christians are getting kicked out of synagogues and their Jewish friends are saying Jesus died a shameful death on the cross, then a big part of what John is doing is setting the record straight. John is telling his audience that opponents of Jesus have the story wrong, and here is the truth to believe.

John shows us that nothing happens *to* Jesus that Jesus doesn't want to happen. Jesus is absolutely in control of everything that happens, including his own death. When we get to that story, we'll see that John tells the story of the passion of Jesus in a way very different from the other Gospels, and Jesus is anything but a victim. John shows that instead of being a hapless victim, Jesus is a victorious Lord. His primary emphasis is not just on Jesus's deity. No, his primary focus is that Jesus is the One you can dare commit your life to, because he wasn't victimized. He made the choice to die and in doing so showed who he is. John is asking Christians to make the choice as well, to follow this Jesus who did not die as a victim of a shameful death but went to the cross by his own choice and the will of the Father.

How did you do with the INTRODUCTORY DARE to skim or read all of John?

Now for this chapter, DARE ONE is to choose one of the stories in the following section titled, "Content Found *Only* in the Gospel of John." As you read, imagine you are in the story, one in the "crowd" who is seeing Jesus, hearing his teaching, and marveling at his miracles. After you read one of the stories, answer the questions in the Truth *and* Dare section below.

Content Found *Only* in the Gospel of John

Source: Felix Just, S.J., PhD (http://catholic-resources.org/John/index .html)

> Prologue (1:1–18)
> Wedding at Cana (2:1–12)
> Nicodemus (2:23–3:21)
> Jesus and/or his disciples baptize people (3:22–26; 4:1–2)
> Samaritan woman at the well (4:1–42)
> Jesus heals a sick man at the Pool of Bethesda (5:1–18)
> New details at the feeding of the five thousand (6:1b, 3–6, 8–9, 12b, 1415)
> Bread of life (6:22–65)
> Woman caught in adultery (7:53–8:11)
> Jesus gives sight to a man born blind (9:1–41)
> Jesus raises Lazarus from the dead (11:1–44)
> Jesus washes the disciples' feet (13:1–20)
> "Disciple whom Jesus loved" (13:23–25; 19:26–27; 20:2–10; 21:7, 20–24; cf. 18:15–16?)
> Last Supper discourses, including "Paraclete" and "Vine and Branches" (13:31–16:33)
> Great prayer of Jesus (17:1–26)
> New details at the trial before Pilate (18:28–19:16)
> New details at the crucifixion (19:20–24, 26–28,30–37, 39)
> First resurrection appearance to Mary Magdalene alone (20:11–18; cf. Matt. 28:9)
> Resurrection appearance to Thomas (20:24–29)
> Another resurrection appearance at the Sea of Tiberias/ Galilee (21:1–25)
> Dialogue between Jesus and Peter (21:1–25; cf. Luke 5:1–11)
> First and second endings to John's Gospel (20:30–31; 21:24–25)

Content Found in Synoptics but Omitted from John

1. Virgin birth
2. Baptism
3. Temptation
4. Parables
5. Transfiguration
6. Lord's Supper as Passover instituted
7. Agony in the Garden
8. Ascension

TRUTH & DARE

DARE ONE

Choose one of the above unique stories in John then discuss the following.

1. What do you like about the story?
2. What do you not like about story?
3. What do you think the story is saying to the audience that originally received it?
4. What is the story saying to us today?
5. What is the story calling us to believe?
6. What is the story calling us to do?
7. With whom can you share this story this week?

DARE TWO:
The Word

*"[In John] Jesus is depicted as the love of God, coming
to dwell among human beings to bring them his divine
truth. He teaches the crowds and seeks out individuals,
especially among the marginalized who respond to him
in faith. Unfortunately, this mission also provokes hostile
reactions [that] lead to his death on the cross."*

—Richard Burridge, Imitating Jesus

AS TEACHERS AND PREACHERS, WE'VE SPENT MUCH
of our lives in libraries and bookstores. Take us to a hardware
store, and we'll flop around like fish on the shore. Drop us amid
rows and rows of books and, aaah, we're swimming.

We've read millions of words. In fact, you could say that
words have been our lives. In Randy's garage is a pile of book
boxes that ranks as the highest manmade point in Abilene,
Texas. So when John starts his Gospel with the most famous,
immortal words of any Gospel, "In the beginning was the
Word," he's got our attention.

The Gospel of Mark starts with Jesus's ministry. Matthew
and Luke start with Jesus's birth, but John's peculiar opening

line draws the reader in because it prompts a question: Is it possible that there is a word, one word that makes all the other millions of words we've read irrelevant by comparison? What would such a word be? Could it really exist, *The* Word? What would it mean for something, or better yet, *someone*, to be that Word?

Lots of ink has been spilled explaining 1:1–18, so we offer only a brief angle on the reading, then we invite you to read the text with this perspective in mind.

Word in Greek is *Logos*. The term *Logos* in John's time would have at least two meanings. One of them is Stoic. The *Logos* is the logic that holds the world together. We don't think that's the prime significance for John. We think the passage so echoes the first book of the Bible, Genesis, that it surely must be what John is trying to get us to think about. Genesis 1:1–2 says, "In the beginning God created the heavens and the earth. Now the earth was formless and empty, darkness was over the surface of the deep, and the Spirit of God was hovering over the waters."

> In the beginning was the Word, and the Word was with God, and the Word was God. He was with God in the beginning. Through him all things were made; without him nothing was made that has been made. In him was life, and that life was the light of all mankind. The light shines in the darkness, and the darkness has not overcome it.
>
> There was a man sent from God whose name was John. He came as a witness to testify concerning that

light, so that through him all might believe. He himself was not the light; he came only as a witness to the light.

The true light that gives light to everyone was coming into the world. He was in the world, and though the world was made through him, the world did not recognize him. He came to that which was his own, but his own did not receive him. Yet to all who did receive him, to those who believed in his name, he gave the right to become children of God—children born not of natural descent, nor of human decision or a husband's will, but born of God.

The Word became flesh and made his dwelling among us. We have seen his glory, the glory of the one and only Son, who came from the Father, full of grace and truth.

(John testified concerning him. He cried out, saying, "This is the one I spoke about when I said, 'He who comes after me has surpassed me because he was before me.'") Out of his fullness we have all received grace in place of grace already given. For the law was given through Moses; grace and truth came through Jesus Christ. No one has ever seen God, but the one and only Son, who is himself God and is in closest relationship with the Father, has made him known. (1:1–18)

The Word of God brings everything into existence. John uses this reference to the *Logos* to indicate that Jesus is the very Word of God, now in the world, in the flesh. Imagine that God wants to communicate with humans. He has an enormous problem.

Randy tells the following story to illustrate how difficult communication is between God and humanity.

In one of my former lives I was a bus minister. What that means is that we'd go and pick up little kids on an old school bus with the word "JOY" painted on the side and take them to church. JOY stood for putting Jesus first, Others second, and Yourself last.

We picked up a child on my bus one day, and he is standing at the back of the bus. The first rule of being a bus minister is there's no standing on the bus, because standing leads to falling, falling leads to bleeding, and bleeding leads to problems. I yell to the kid, "Okay, sit down. The bus is getting ready to leave."

He ignores me.

I say a little louder, "The bus is getting ready to leave. Sit down." He ignores me. I say really loud, "You better sit down. The bus is getting ready to leave."

Finally some other child from the back of the bus says, "He can't hear you, he's deaf." I said, "What?" She said, "He's deaf! What's the matter, you deaf too?"

Okay, I've got it, so I go and scoop him up, and I bring him up to the front of the bus with me. He's probably three and he's deaf. We're going to have an hour-long bus ride. I'm thinking, how am I going to communicate with this little guy? How am I going to keep him entertained for the next hour? I think to myself, we'll do sign language. Well, he doesn't know how to sign. Actually, I don't know how to sign either, so that's not going to work.

We'll pass notes. He's three; he can't read. I've got nothing here.

The gap between God and me is much larger than the gap between this little guy and me.

God's got a problem. We've got an even bigger problem unless God solves his problem.

Now, when God's having a conversation among the Trinity of Father, Son, and Holy Spirit, we don't know what kind of language they speak. We're guessing it's some sort of Vulcan, Star Trek mind-meld. But if God's going to speak to us, he has to come down to our level, because we have no way to get to his, so the words come ringing: *The Word was made flesh so we could understand him on our level.*

But misunderstanding God was just as common then as it is now. We get this recurring theme in John where Jesus says in a variety of different ways, "If you've seen me you've seen the Father." The book of John is going to be all about God's effort to let us see who he really is. One way to get at who Jesus is, who he claims to be, who the prophets, including John the Baptist, claimed Jesus to be is to look at the titles used for Jesus in the Gospel of John.

Read John 1:19–51, and check in the margin of your Bible or in a journal each time you see a title or a claim about who Jesus is. John the Baptist calls him the "Lamb of God who takes away the sin of the world." Jewish people would not miss this reference to Passover, that the blood of a lamb painted on the door frame of their homes was the sign for the death angel to pass over their houses and not kill the firstborn child of each home in Egypt in the days of Moses.

Would they follow this teacher until they realized that the time when he was crucified, according to John, was on

Passover? Would they realize that the Lamb of God was a new liberator of Israel? Robert Kysar, whose book, *The Maverick Gospel* influenced us greatly, says, "The Lamb of God is the liberating revealer of God. His freeing function occurs not strictly through his suffering and death but through his very person. To know him is to be freed."

Kysar claims, and we agree, that God's incarnation is *part* of the freedom from sin we experience. Christians often focus mainly on the atonement of Christ, his blood shed on the cross for our sins, as the way God saves us. But God was saving before Christ, redeeming Israel, saving through Christ's incarnation and life, saving through his death, saving through his resurrection, reign, and return someday.

S. D. Gordon says what Jesus did in coming to us was a "divine errand of love." His very presence is freedom and forgiveness. He freely forgives people he encounters in the Gospel story.

Another important title is "Son of Man." The title makes little sense to modern readers, but it's important we learn more to understand how significant this title is to the identity of Jesus. Granted, titles can say a grand total of zero. Take the title "president." This title doesn't say much of anything about who the person really is. Likewise, the title Son of Man doesn't really tell us much about Jesus. In fact, Augustus Caesar in Greek documents was called "Emperor Caesar Augustus, Son of God." This may sound like Augustus is delusional, but it really tells us little about him.

If we want to understand what Son of Man means in reference to Jesus, then we need to look at how the phrase is used in the Gospel of John, where various forms of Son of Man, Son, and Son of God are used more than all the other Gospels combined. Look up John 3:13–17; 5:19–27; 6:16–38; 12:23–49, and notice the references to the Son.

Son of Man is important less because it's a title and more because of the relationship the designation points to with "The Father." To understand John, it's imperative we understand the relationship connection between Jesus and the One he calls "the Father."

Kysar says, "The Son of Man and Son titles constitute the heart of Johannine Christology." Kysar points out that John does a creative wonder by bringing together Hebrew and Hellenistic thought about sonship. For Jews, to be a good son is to obey commands of God. That's what it means to be a son of God. For Greeks, son is a cosmic matter, which is more difficult for most of us to get than the Jewish idea. To quote one of our college students, "Like, what does that even mean?"

Remember Mythology 101? To be sons of god was to be birthed by the gods. For Greeks, sonship is all about the origin and nature of a person. For Jews, on the other hand, sonship is about what a son does, his obedience. John brings both of those ideas together masterfully. Jesus obeys the Father, yes (4:34), but he also is the essence of the Father, though he is not created (10:30).

This obedient Sonship of Jesus to the Father is primarily about a relationship, yet this relationship is the one thing we often overlook in reading the story. The upshot of all this is that Jesus invites us into that relationship. You'll see that invitation repeated throughout this book, because if there's one thing we want to do here, it's to be sure we are all aware that when we follow Jesus, he invites us into this same kind of relationship with the Father. Kysar poetically calls the incarnate Christ "the stairway between heaven and earth."

That's why we're digging deeply into what Sonship in John means for Jesus and the Father, so that we can more fully participate in the divine-human relationship. Jesus fully participates in the being of God, yet he is also individual and can be seen and touched—he's a real human being, not just a creature who seems to be human or shape-shifting. This confused the disciples even as they were seeing and touching him.

In addition to the relationship of Son to the Father, other titles also help us understand the relationship between Jesus and the Father through the Spirit. This relationship of Father, Son, and Holy Spirit, in turn, helps us understand God's relationship to us, and finally helps us understand human relationships.

Jesus was called Teacher, and that title would have brought to mind people like Socrates and Plato, but Jesus shatters stereotypes. The Teacher was no mere philosopher. The Word was no mere philosophy. The Son of Man was no mere king. All three of these roles were common: teacher, philosopher, and king. Neither Jesus himself nor John seemed to be inventing new titles or designations for Jesus. John used symbols, metaphors, and titles that meant something to people in his day; then he turned these ideas on their heads. The idea of *Logos* was not a new idea in the Greek world. Caesars were called Son of God. You could swing a scroll and hit teachers on every street corner in Greek and Roman cities.

But in Christ, the Son of Man is the servant of all.

The Word becomes flesh.

The Teacher leaves students with another Counselor, the Holy Spirit to teach disciples further.

The Word is not an idea or philosophy but a person. Wisdom is personified. Jesus didn't come to bring wisdom. Jesus *is* wisdom. He is Lord, yet he comes not to lord over people but to wash their feet, the work of a slave.

John wants us to know that if we really want to see God, look at Jesus. In 14:8–10, Philip pleads, "Show us the Father, and that will be enough for us." Jesus seems exasperated by this time with his disciple and replies, "Don't you know me, Philip, even after I have been among you such a long time? Anyone who has seen me has seen the Father. How can you say, 'Show us the Father'? Don't you believe that I am in the Father, and that the Father is in me? The words I say to you I do not speak on my own authority. Rather, it is the Father, living in me, who is doing his work."

Jesus has been hanging out with God forever, literally. The Father and Jesus are so close that John can write not only that "the Word was *with* God," but he can also say, "The Word *was* God."

Most of us have had the experience of having somebody give us a recommendation. Who do you want to give you a recommendation? You want someone who knows you best. They can best reveal who you really are. Likewise, Jesus is revealing the Father, so Jesus is the best reference we could have.

So we have this recurring theme in John: Jesus was with the Father. He's the one who's come down from heaven. The

Father and I are one. God is in the flesh for us to see. God is communicating to us in a way that we are able to get it.

But the disciples didn't always get it. And neither do we. Over and over the disciples, the Jews, the crowd see Jesus and the signs he performs, and they eat the food he feeds them, but they still don't understand. The disciples, the crowds, and the Jews make a really good foil for us as readers. Raymond Brown compares this with Arthur Conan Doyle's Sherlock Holmes and Dr. Watson. Holmes's sidekick, Watson, is the foil for the reader. Watson and the reader think they have things figured out, then they are surprised to learn that Sherlock Holmes has quite another angle on the matter.

Likewise when we read John, we think we have it figured out, and we cluck our tongues at the stubborn disciples. Then by the end of the story we're scratching our heads as well. John has done his job. He's shown us that God can be seen in Jesus, yet misunderstood by humanity, and until we come to our own crisis of misunderstanding, we may be following a God who is much too fashioned in our own image and limited understanding.

One of the saddest lines in John comes early on in 1:10: "He was in the world, and though the world was made through him, the world did not recognize him."

Imagine the pain of un-recognition that families feel when they care for a mother, father, or spouse with Alzheimer's. Mothers and fathers of infants long for the day when their baby will lock eyes on them in recognition. For those caring for a disabled, sick, or malnourished baby, the look of recognition never comes.

We imagine the old disciple Jesus loved saddened as he writes, "He came to that which was his own, but his own did not receive him." For the most part, humanity never locked eyes on its Creator-in-the-flesh.

The sadness of un-recognition will not deter Jesus, however, but will lead him to reveal himself in a way that humans would finally acknowledge. He would die for us. And for those who received this message, John says we can then receive the same kind of family relationship that the Father and the Son have. "Yet to all who did receive him, to those who believed in his name, he gave the right to become children of God—children born not of natural descent, nor of human decision or a husband's will, but born of God."

S. D. Gordon tells a story about this sadness of un-recognition.

There was once a woman in England who had to work as a maid after her husband died, and the young boy she was raising alone was a favorite around the estate where she worked. The owner of the estate became very fond of the boy and sent him to boarding school, university, and medical school. The boy became a man, skilled as a doctor, famous, then wealthy and lived in London, some distance from the smaller village where his mother still worked on the estate. He remembered his dear old mother, of course, and he sent her money, fabric for dresses, and wrote her letters. In the busy absorption of his life, however, it had been a long time since he'd traveled to see his mother.

The sweet old woman lived with a consciousness that her son was doing good work in London. When the neighbors stopped in, her "Laddie," she called him, was always a topic of conversation. She would tell of the nice letters he wrote, the much too fancy fabric for her plain tastes, and she would always end almost talking into her tea and to no one in particular, "but I wish, I just wish I could see my Laddie."

Years passed and things changed at the estate. The owner died, and the estate had to be sold to pay debts. The old woman would have to make new arrangements. It was no time until she knew exactly what she would do. "I'll go up to London and live with Laddie!" But in her mind she thought it best not to send word but to go up and surprise her son, the doctor, who by now was still living alone in a grand house. He would have plenty of space and it would be delightful for them both.

And so she went. It was her first train ride to London, and even after she arrived, she would have to inquire about how to find her son's address. Night had fallen by the time she made it to the beautiful house, and she knocked on the door. She smoothed her coat and dress she had made from the fabric her Laddie had sent years before, and could not contain the smile on her face just thinking about the surprise about to happen when Laddie opened the door.

In place of her son, a butler opened the door. The woman was taken back a little but asked, "Is Lad—uh, is the doctor in?" The butler did not know the woman and explained that the doctor could not see her since it was after hours. When he resisted showing her in, the woman set her jaw and said through gritted teeth, "I'll see the doctor."

At this the butler asked the woman to wait while he went to report about this strangely insistent woman at the door. The doctor agreed to see her. The doctor was indeed surprised to see his old sweet mother, and they embraced long and warmly.

"How did you happen to come? And why didn't you send word?"

"I wanted to surprise you," the woman said, taking off her coat.

The doctor asked the butler to bring tea and soon they were sitting by a warm fire sipping English tea and filling in the blank places where years, fewer visits and letters left gaping holes.

As she sat sipping her tea, she unraveled the story of the estate and ended with, "And now I'm coming to live with you, Laddie."

The doctor was poking the fire and listening to his mother talk. He thought of his friends, his civic and work duties, the dinners he held at his home with sophisticated city servants. As he listened to his mother's old country twang, he thought how he'd never really noticed it before, but now it grated strangely. It certainly wouldn't do to have her come live with him. But as quickly as that thought came, a tide rose in his heart and he realized what a cad he was being. Of course, he thought, she's my mother, and if my mother wants to come here, then here she comes. But as he continued to think and poke the fire, he could not bring himself to welcome her to his home.

"Mother, you know it is not very healthful here in the city. We have bad fogs in London. You are used to the country air. It wouldn't agree with you here, I'm afraid. I'll get you a little cottage on the edge of town, and I'll come and see you very often."

"It's a bit late, Laddie, I'm thinking, to talk about new plans."

And he said softly, "Forgive me, mother. It's late, yes." And he showed her to her room to sleep.

The doctor always rose early, and after some time he expected his mother would excitedly be down for some tea and more conversation. But she had woken much earlier, gathered her things, and left before her Laddie woke. She had thought to herself, *It doesn't suit my Laddie's plans to have me here. I don't understand why not, but it isn't his fault. It just doesn't suit. I'll never be a trouble to my Laddie.*

The doctor looked at the train station for his mother but did not find her. He continued to search for her in the city and asked about her in the surrounding countryside. He even went back to his home village, expecting to find her there, but people had not seen her since the day she left for London to see her "Laddie."

Months passed, and a woman came into the hospital after a street accident, and it was the doctor's mother. Even under the dire circumstances, he was happy to see her, and he attended to his unconscious mother and instructed all his staff to give her the best of care.

She came to her own, and her own received her not. He loved her, but it didn't suit his plans.

Jesus came to his own, and his own received him not. It didn't suit their plans. Ah! listen yet further: He comes to his own, you and me, and his own—you finish it. Have we some plans, too, set plans, that we don't intend to change, even for— (softly now)—even him? Each of us is finishing that sentence, not in words so much if at all, in words of our action.

Gordon's story helps us feel what John may have felt when he wrote about his friend Jesus, "He came unto his own, but his own did not receive him." It must have saddened John to write those words, but is it any less sad when we continue to make our plans with no room for the One who gave birth to our faith?

James Bryan Smith uses the wonderful phrase, "coming to know the God that Jesus knows." We could cinch up the belt one more notch and say, "We're invited to know the God that Jesus *is.*" This invitation is not only to learn the titles we've discussed or the "I Am" statements of Jesus in the Gospel of John, but to also be invited into the deep community these "I Am" statements point to.

Many scholars think that repeatedly saying "I Am" is Jesus's way of indicating that he and God are one. Those of you who know a little language know that many languages are highly inflected and English is not. If I want to say "I Am" in English, I need two words. In Greek, you just need one word. All you really need is the word "Am." That word sufficiently says "I Am." The verb "to be."

Frequently with John when you have these "I Am" statements, you don't have one word; you have two. The first word in Greek that means "I" is really not necessary: "*ego eimi.*" We translate this, "I Am." You may have to go back and read these sentences again! We did. Some scholars think that when Jesus uses this phrase, he wants you to be thinking about the moment when Moses stood before a burning bush in the wilderness, amazed. God identified himself: "I Am." Does Jesus mean for his hearers to think of him as the same God who identified himself to Moses as "I Am"?

The *Logos* and the "I Am" statements in John are doing the same thing. They are giving Jesus credentials for being the One who shows us who God is. If you really want to know who God is, you stare at Jesus, because he can truthfully say, "The Father and I are one." We've been together for eternity. I'm the One who is fully qualified to reveal God to you.

We recommend you find on your media service or purchase and listen to the Michael Card song, "The Final Word."

Card has written lyrics and music that bring the biblical story off the page in a way that is in itself incarnational: word becomes music and dwells in our hearts and on our lips. The following lines of Card's song hint at the beauty and mystery of the incarnation.

> *And so the Light became alive*
> *And manna became Man.*
> *Eternity stepped into time*
> *So we could understand.*
> *He spoke the Incarnation and then so was born the Son.*
> *His final Word was Jesus, He needed no other one.*
> *Spoke flesh and blood so He could bleed and make a*
> *way Divine.*
> *And so was born the baby who would die to make*
> *it mine.*

We love preaching in African-American churches. When we preach in white churches, we talk and people listen. But when we preach in African-American churches, the listeners talk back to us. And when we say something the congregation really likes, sometimes someone will shout out, "Now that's getting it said!"

Now, we see what John is after. In Jesus Christ, God got it said. All the words that have ever been written can't tell us as much about God as the living embodiment, Jesus Christ. But when we see Jesus, we see the Final Word, and we see what happens when God really gets it said.

He Still Turns Water to Wine

It's embarrassing for a hostess when the food runs out before the appetites of the guests. We have friends who tell the following story about that embarrassment.

The family had been called together shortly before the guests arrived. Mom informed the children that under no circumstances were they to eat more than one piece of chicken. There simply was not enough for everyone to have two, and any extra pieces were for the visitors. The guests arrived, all sat down to dinner, and that chicken was gooooood, said the oldest male guest in an Andy Griffith or Cousin Eddie sort of way.

The host family's youngest boy, Pat, ate his drumstick and really wanted another piece. He couldn't understand why the one-piece rule had been inflicted when the plate was stacked with more pieces, and everyone looked like they were happily eating. Maybe he could get a piece without his mother noticing? Crazy talk, his mother could see what he was doing from upstairs, around three corners with two doors shut between them. She'd see him take the chicken. So Pat watched the guests eat more chicken. The oldest male guest ate his first and second pieces, then asked for more, because it was gooood. Pat watched every bite the guest took, and played with his mashed potatoes. Then it happened. He couldn't believe it. The guest went for a fourth piece of chicken! Pat couldn't contain himself when the guest stuck the fork in his fourth piece. Pat let out a gutteral growl toward the guest and said, "Ya HOG!"

Jesus went with his mother and some of his disciples to a wedding in Cana of Galilee. Weddings in those days usually ran several days. There was a procession around the village so everyone could bless the new couple. The bride and groom didn't rush off to their honeymoon but stayed in the home several days, holding court and being served like king and queen. For a village, this was entertainment, joy, and a welcome celebration in the midst of the hardships of life.

Then the nightmare of every host happened. Provisions ran low, then ran totally out. In this case, the wineskins were empty. No wine was left for guests. This was a situation that was somewhat worse than the sweet iced tea and the fresh squeezed lemonade running out in the Atlanta Chick-fil-A.

Embarrassment wafted over the party like a bad smell. The wine wasn't a choice of drinks. It was *the* drink. When the wine supply was too short for the length of the wedding, joy drained away with the last drop. You can read about the embarrassment in John 2:1–11.

Mary wanted Jesus to do something about the poor family's shame, and Jesus on the face of it seemed to give the average male response: "Woman, what does this have to do with me?" Jesus had his reasons. One of them seemed to be the timing of his ministry launch, but his mother seems to either ignore this or she so trusted him to do whatever he saw fit. So she said to the servants, "Do whatever he tells you."

Because of all the problems alcohol has caused over the years, some Christians might be happier with Jesus's miracle if he'd changed wine to water! But Jesus has other plans. He asks the servants to fill six water jars used for ceremonial washing and then dip some out. When they gave it to the master of the banquet, he tasted it and was surprised. He didn't know where this wine came from, but the servants knew. He called the groom aside and observed that usually when people were good and drunk, most hosts brought out the cheaper wine, but he had saved the best for last!

John records this wedding miracle Jesus did because of his mother's sympathy for friends who were about to face the stinging embarrassment of running out of wine at a wedding. We could say that Jesus did this miracle because his mama told him to, but she didn't really. Being what some people call Jesus's first disciple, Mary shows us early on in the Gospel what it's like to want your way but to resign yourself to "do what he says." At the end of the story, John says this sign of changing water to wine revealed

Jesus's glory. The result was that many disciples put their faith in him. This translation in the NIV is one of the better ways to render the verb *faith*, what we've been calling "faithing" or "daring faith."

The water-to-wine story is rich and meaningful, and we could stop there, but with John, we always have to consider the deeper meaning of what's happening in the stories. For Greeks, the story of Jesus changing the water to wine would not be the first time they'd heard such a tale. They would have heard of Dionysus and the Midas touch that could turn water to wine and things into gold. Jews, on the other hand, would notice in the story something we completely miss: Jesus used twenty-to-thirty-gallon water jars reserved for ceremonial washing. For Jews, the question had always been, "Am I pure enough? Am I clean or unclean? Have I washed properly? Have I kept the Sabbath?" Some call this a replacement miracle, which seems to signal an end or replacement of ceremonial holiness with wine of celebration of the presence of God-on-earth.

Lots of preachers say this story is about God's abundance and extravagance toward us. Granted, over one hundred fifty gallons of wine could never be consumed by a wedding party, but is God's extravagant love and abundance a too-quick American interpretation? Lots of cultures celebrate like this with what seems to be an endless supply of wine and food. Later in John's Gospel, he shows Jesus very thirsty on a journey through Samaria, and on the cross he's thirsty again. Even for Jesus himself, there is no abundance of drink. He's not shown in John 2 to be a winebibber or a party animal. God surely gives in abundance, but I don't think that's the main theme of this story. Jesus is compassionate toward his mother and her close friends who were ashamed to have guests and not have the means to host them. He does a miracle that has obvious meaning for those who knew the difference between ceremonial washing jars and wine containers. Something was up, and it's hard to imagine that the first readers sat back and satisfied themselves with the explanation that God sure is a God who gives aplenty.

When we visited families in villages in Uganda, particularly when my wife and children were along or we'd take guests from the United States, we'd often stop to buy sugar, flour, bread, milk, or meat to take to the people who would be hosting us for the day. While we didn't want to steal that beautiful dignity of their sacrificial hospitality, we also didn't want poor families to feel the need to do what is common for unexpected guests: borrow money or supplies to host visitors. Jesus had his disciples with him. They may have been extras at the wedding. Were they part of the reason the wine ran out?

William Barclay tells a story about Sir Wilfred Grenfell appealing for missionaries in Labrador many years ago. Grenfell said to the missionary recruits: "I cannot promise you much money. I can promise you the time of your life!"

What if the story of the wedding is less about abundance and more about John's memory of what it's like to be with Jesus? In the presence of Jesus, water turns to wine. Does John want us to see that Jesus still turns water to wine when he enters a person's life? Ceremonial washing turns to wine of forgiveness. Law keeping turns to grace.

Jesus doesn't simply produce the wine from nothing. He performs his first miracle through the hands of slaves. Like those slaves or slaves to religious law, do we have any legalistic tendencies; any water of the old life that we need to fill up in those jars and let Jesus change to wine? Are you willing to fill up your jars of ceremonial water and let Jesus do a miracle? To let Jesus turn your legalism to grace? Can he turn the religious, judging knots in your stomach to a relaxed, joyful, serving life, your water to wine? What are the jars you need to fill up and let Jesus change?

—Greg

TRUTH & DARE

DARE TWO

Read John 1

1. What do you like about the story?
2. What do you not like about story?
3. What do you think the story is saying to the audience that originally received it?
4. What is the story saying to us today?
5. What is the story calling us to believe?
6. What is the story calling us to do?
7. With whom can you share this story this week?

DARE THREE:
Born Again

"It was wonderful being born again, but I don't think my
mother enjoyed it very much."
—John Wing

IN THE BOOK OF JOHN, WE FIND A WHOLE SERIES
of encounters people have with Jesus that aren't recorded in any
other Gospel. If there is a slogan about conversations between
Jesus and these people he meets, it might be this: "When Jesus
talks, people misunderstand."

The first of these encounter stories is with a man named
Nicodemus (John 3). As you read the following story, would
you consider these questions? How does John describe
Nicodemus? When does John say Nicodemus comes to Jesus?
What does Nicodemus say after Jesus speaks about being born
of the Spirit?

Now there was a Pharisee, a man named Nicodemus who was a member of the Jewish ruling council. He came to Jesus at night and said, "Rabbi, we know that you are a teacher who has come from God. For no one could perform the signs you are doing if God were not with him."

Jesus replied, "Very truly I tell you, no one can see the kingdom of God unless they are born again."

"How can someone be born when they are old?" Nicodemus asked. "Surely they cannot enter a second time into their mother's womb to be born!"

Jesus answered, "Very truly I tell you, no one can enter the kingdom of God unless they are born of water and the Spirit. Flesh gives birth to flesh, but the Spirit gives birth to spirit. You should not be surprised at my saying, 'You must be born again.' The wind blows wherever it pleases. You hear its sound, but you cannot tell where it comes from or where it is going. So it is with everyone born of the Spirit."

"How can this be?" Nicodemus asked.

"You are Israel's teacher," said Jesus, "and do you not understand these things? Very truly I tell you, we speak of what we know, and we testify to what we have seen, but still you people do not accept our testimony. I have spoken to you of earthly things and you do not believe; how then will you believe if I speak of heavenly things? No one has ever gone into heaven except the one who came from heaven—the Son of Man. Just as Moses lifted up the snake in the wilderness, so the Son of Man must

be lifted up, that everyone who believes may have eternal
life in him."

For God so loved the world that he gave his one
and only Son, that whoever believes in him shall not
perish but have eternal life. For God did not send his
Son into the world to condemn the world, but to save
the world through him. Whoever believes in him is
not condemned, but whoever does not believe stands
condemned already because they have not believed in
the name of God's one and only Son. This is the verdict:
Light has come into the world, but people loved darkness
instead of light because their deeds were evil. Everyone
who does evil hates the light, and will not come into the
light for fear that their deeds will be exposed. But whoever lives by the truth comes into the light, so that it may
be seen plainly that what they have done has been done
in the sight of God. (3:1–21)

The Nicodemus story gives context to the most famous verse in
the New Testament: John 3:16. What comes after this famous
verse brings the story back around to where it began: in darkness. Jesus comes not just to shed light on Nicodemus's dark
and earth-bound understanding, but he comes to save the
world from this darkness. The whole story expands to show
what happens if we accept or deny this truth Jesus brings
from above.

Nicodemus came at night. The story of Nicodemus is
bookended with darkness. John observes that people love
darkness. We have a hard time coming out of darkness into

the light. This is a reference carried on later in John as Jesus comments about spiritual blindness. This is Nicodemus's story. Nicodemus has religious pedigree as a Pharisee, a religious man's religious man. If three-piece suits, pompadours, and tie bars with American flags, a cross, and a leather-bound nine-pound Bible had been available, Nicodemus would have been sporting and schlepping it all. He's a back-to-the-Bible fundamentalist, but he approaches Jesus secretly. He is struggling in the twilight between darkness and light.

Just as Christians today cling to big-time preachers, so also Nicodemus is star-struck with the new rabbi who is beginning to dazzle people with his teaching and miraculous signs. Nicodemus has seen Jesus performing miracles (or at least heard of them), and on that basis he confesses to Jesus that he believes Jesus is from God. Earlier in 2:23–24, John told us that Jesus did not value signs-based faith, and Jesus replies to Nicodemus by saying that his way of religious thinking won't work in the world Jesus comes to reveal.

Could it be that Nicodemus represents an exploratory committee to recruit Jesus into the cause of restoring Judaism? Nicodemus certainly has an agenda that includes others, for he begins with "we know." Nicodemus is confident and seems to have a religious agenda unlike anything Jesus has in mind. Jesus's agenda is "from above" and contrasts with what Nicodemus's agenda from below may be. It seems Jesus is calling Nicodemus to change his way of thinking as a religious leader.

Some scholars say the proper way to translate "you must be born again" would instead be "you must be born from above." It's not uncommon to have differences on how Greek or Hebrew words get translated into English. That's one reason why we have so many English translations. The translation of "born from above" seems to match and make more sense of Jesus's response. When Nicodemus concludes that because Jesus does signs he is "from above," Jesus responds that Nicodemus too must be "re-born from above." Whether the translation is "born again" or "born from above," the point seems to be that Nicodemus must begin to think like someone with a relationship to the Father, rather than someone who is more interested in relationships with things of earth such as the law, religion, wealth, security, and reputation.

These are the currencies of the kingdom for Nicodemus. Dazzle me with signs, and I'll dazzle you with my religious pedigree. But now Jesus has this religious expert scratching his head. Jesus says you must be born again, and Nicodemus takes him literally and argues about how impossible it is to enter again into the womb of your mother. This isn't in the text, but we think Jesus rolls his eyes here. Later, in some frustration, he says, "You are Israel's teacher and you don't understand these things?"

Maybe you are Nicodemus. We are. Your parents and grandparents were Christians. You grew up in Christian homes. You are in the "right" political party that holds all the correct religious views, and being a Christian is the most natural thing in the world.

Others of you are seeking Jesus or are more recent converts. You have come to Jesus later in your life. You may not have come from a Christian family at all. Occasionally in church groups you're frustrated because people seem to know things you don't know about the Bible or religion.

Religious people like us don't like it when we can't understand something about God or the Bible. We expect to have God, the Bible, and our views all settled. And when someone like Jesus comes along and upends our religious equilibrium, as he did to Nicodemus, we blow a fuse. We start grasping, as Nicodemus did.

When Jesus speaks about the Spirit of God and being born of Spirit and water, Nicodemus is dumbstruck. What is all this mystical talk about blowing wind? Jesus says that's how it is with the Spirit of God and people born from above. We don't get to dictate to him where the wind blows!

Nicodemus must have been scratching his head under his turban, because he says, "How can this be?"

What's Jesus trying to tell Nicodemus? If we were guessing, and that's really all anyone can do with the story, we would say this: Everybody comes into the Kingdom of God in the same way. You come in as a baby. You don't get to bring your reputation, religious pedigree, biblical knowledge, and self-importance. Everybody's got to come in the same way.

The next story John is going to tell is likely no accident of order. He tells us next about a woman with a negative pedigree. John has arranged the stories together so we understand that it doesn't matter where you start, it doesn't matter what your religious credentials are. The first thing you have to do is realize that you are totally dependent on God. Furthermore, you should know that God's Spirit moves wherever he wants to, and here's what you and all of us have to say about it: nothing.

We don't get to choose where God's Spirit moves. Remember the movie, *Amadeus*, about Mozart and his rival, Antonio Salieri? Salieri chaffed that God would place his musical gift in a person as annoying as Mozart! If we had our choice and got to choose who was in the church and who wasn't, some of you wouldn't make it. If we could vote you off the island, you'd be gone. And by now, you've had enough time to get annoyed at us or to disagree enough with us to vote us off the island, too.

So here is Nicodemus, top of the religious tree, and it is as if Jesus is saying to him, "If you want to be in good with God, it's going to be because the Spirit of God calls you, not because you have such a great religious pedigree. You must be born again."

Many people read the phrase "you must be born again" as a reference to baptism. This mention of water is one of twenty references to water in John's story. Are these references to water accidental or somehow connected? Does Jesus point beyond physical water in discussing water with Nicodemus and the Samaritan woman? Do these references point to something beyond the actual water? We believe they do. It's natural for Christians to think of baptism when Jesus says, "You must be born again," but if we get stuck thinking only about baptism in this story, we've missed the boat. Or at least we're in the boat of misunderstanding with Nicodemus. At least he was scratching his head. If we're sure we have it right and it's only about baptism, then we've done little with the story other than replacing Nicodemus's legalism for ours. When Jesus speaks of being born again, he's more likely aiming at a reality of a relationship that Jesus makes available to humans who are "born of the Spirit." In other words, the Spirit gives us connectivity with the Father, just as Jesus has.

One of our friends was officiating at his son's wedding. How awkward to do your own son's wedding! He told the bride and groom, "Your parents have prayed from the moment of your birth for that right person to come along to be your husband or wife. Your parents have been trying to help you become the kind of person who would find that right person." Then he said to the bride and groom, "Your true identity does not have anything to do with who you were born to, or where you were born, or when you were born. Your true identity has to do with when you were born again. When you said yes to God, that changed everything."

I don't know what Nicodemus was thinking when he went to see Jesus. As we find out in the book of John, Jesus speaks quite negatively about the Jewish religious leaders. In Nicodemus's case, we have a very curious Jewish leader. Jesus makes it clear that if you think that what he's about is one more Jewish law thing, you've got it wrong. He's offering something entirely new. If John is showing us that Christianity is not just an odd sort of Judaism, but it is something else entirely, then we see why he included this story. It's not enough to be a good Jew. You have to see in Jesus the One who's going to lead you to life. And for Christians today, we're saying, be careful not to repeat the mistake of making this about new forms of legalism or your reputation or works as a Christian servant.

What does this story mean then? Jesus asks Nicodemus this question. He says, "You're a teacher of Israel and you don't get this?" Because your religious identity doesn't have to do with how much religion you study. It has to do with whether you recognize Jesus as the Word, the Way, the Truth, the Life, the Living Water, the Giver of New Birth. That's what determines your true religious identity. You're a teacher of Israel and you don't understand this? It's the power and the Spirit of God, not your position, that matters. When you come into the Kingdom of God, everybody comes the same way. Everybody comes on equal footing. Everybody comes in as a totally dependent baby. So Jesus says to Nicodemus.

Two themes can been seen here: one theme is the move from self-reliance to God-reliance, becoming born again as a baby who is dependent on a mother. The second theme is the need for Nicodemus—and for all who follow Jesus—to move from undercover out into the light from above, to a daring faith. As David Fleer puts it, Nicodemus will move in the story of John from certitude to mystery to discipleship. This means we will see him again in later chapters (see the sidebar later in this book).

None of us have God figured out. Maybe we have a thimbleful of understanding of God with a few oceans left to dip out. For now, Nicodemus is still undercover and scratching his head. It's not a bad thing to be scratching. That itch for God is part of what it means to be human.

Entering as Children

Recently, at dawn, I made a visit with some friends to one of my favorite places on earth—the baptismal pool on the Abilene Christian University campus. Every time I'm here, I think about the last student I baptized here—how he looked when he came up out of the water and his friends greeted him. It also makes me think about my own baptism. Almost all of us recall what it was like when we came out of the water at our baptism.

One of the things in our world we really value is expertise. Almost all of us want to be an expert in something. We want people to admire our ability in some area. But Jesus makes it clear that when you come into the Kingdom of God, nobody comes in as an expert. We all come in as children. Scholars may debate about what Jesus says to Nicodemus and how it should be translated. Some say that when Jesus says, "You must be born of the water and the Spirit," he is specifically teaching about baptism. But there can be no debate about this: if we're going to come into the Kingdom of God, we're going to come in as children.

—*Randy*

He Must Become Greater, I Must Become Less!

"As we grow older, we tend to become control freaks. We need to control everybody and everything, moment by moment, to be happy. If the now has never been full or sufficient, we will always be grasping, even addictive or obsessive. If you're pushing yourself and others around, you have not yet found the secret of happiness. It's okay as it is. This moment is as perfect as it can be. The saints called it the 'sacrament of the present moment.'" —Richard Rohr, *Everything Belongs*

I recently took a six week sabbatical, and one of the best things I began during the sabbatical was counseling with Terry Ewing of Plumbline Ministries. One of the big issues many of us deal with in counseling is control. The question could be framed this way: Are you God? Or are you not God?

It seems a ridiculous question. Of course, I'm not God. But sometimes we act like we think we are. As Richard Rohr says in the quote above, as we grow older, we tend to want to push ourselves and others around, judge, tell others what they should and shouldn't do. A counseling professor I had years ago called this "should-ing on people." We spout opinions about the way the world should be if we were in charge. We think we're all-knowing because we have a smart phone. We often take on much more responsibility for situations than we ought.

It has been helpful to me to step back from getting emotionally involved in a problem at home or work and ask myself, "Am I God? Can I control this situation?" No. This is the stuff of the "Serenity Prayer" that goes like this (say it with me): "Lord, give me the serenity to accept the things I cannot change." Stop there. This means everyone around you. You can't change people around you. The prayer could helpfully add, "and people" to read, "Lord, give me the serenity to accept the things and people I cannot change." This includes ourselves!

One Sunday I asked the church to repeat, "I am not God." It felt good for some to release the pressure to carry burdens only God can carry for us. I am not God, and as such I do not control the world. I can cry or be pained for the world, lament war, famine, refugees, and do something about it by planning my life around helping the poor, the refugee, and bringing peace wherever I'm present, but I cannot ultimately change the world's situation or carry the burden of the world on my shoulders. I am not God.

A man named John the Baptist made a public confession that he was not God. He had to. He was over-appreciated. People thought he was from above. They thought he was the Messiah. Or they thought he was a prophet come to announce the Messiah. Some people in the days when John the Baptist lived, thought Elijah would come back and herald the coming of the Christ. So it became important for John to proclaim that he was not the Messiah, not God.

When people asked him, "Who are you?" he first said who he was not. "I am not the Messiah. I am not Elijah." Then who are you, John? "I am a voice crying in the wilderness, Repent! I'm preparing the pathway for the Messiah" (1:19–34).

Later, some of his disciples saw Jesus with his disciples baptizing on the other side of the river (3:22–36), and they stirred the pot with John, trying to prompt comparison and competition between John and his cousin Jesus. Here, after already saying who he was not, John went further to describe himself only in relationship to Jesus.

He said something that is golden and rings down through the years to us today as a mantra that could change our churches, our families, our lives.

"He must become greater. I must become less."

NPR's "Morning Edition" tells the story of Julio Diaz, a 31-year-old social worker from New York City who after work one night exited the subway onto a nearly empty platform. As the train left, a boy about twelve years old was standing near Diaz. The boy pulled a knife to threaten Diaz and asked for his money.

Diaz gave the boy his wallet and the boy fled. Before the boy was too far away to hear, Diaz shouted at him, "Wait! You forgot something. Here, take my coat." Diaz was taking off his coat when the boy stopped, turned around, and looked puzzled.

"Are you crazy? Why are you doing this?" the boy asked.

"Well, if you're willing to risk your freedom for a few dollars, then I guess you must really need the money. I mean, all I wanted to do was to get dinner. And, if you want to join me, you're more than welcome."

The boy agreed to join Diaz. They walked to the diner and sat in a booth. Soon the waitress came by and asked Diaz if he'd have the usual. She chatted a few minutes before putting in the order. The manager came by the booth to say hello to Diaz and his young friend. The dishwasher came out to say hello.

Watching all this, the boy asked, "Hey, man, do you own this place?"

"No, why?"

"Because you know everybody."

"I just eat here a lot."

"But you're even nice to the dishwasher."

"Well, haven't you been taught that you should be nice to everybody?" Diaz asked the boy.

"Yeah, but I didn't think people really acted that way," the boy said.

The social worker in Diaz saw an opening. He asked the boy what he really wanted out of life. The boy's face was downcast, and he didn't have much of an answer.

When the bill came, Diaz told the boy, "Look, I guess you're going to have to pay this bill for me, because you have my money, and I can't pay for it. But if you give my wallet back, I'll gladly treat you."

The boy handed over the wallet. Diaz paid the bill, and then he pulled out a twenty-dollar bill, placed it on the table and pushed it across the table to the boy. "I know you could use this, but I want to ask you to give me something in return: your knife."

The boy took the twenty dollars and handed over his knife to Diaz. I don't know what Diaz's beliefs are, but he was living like a man who had a mantra like John the Baptist's: He must become greater. I must become less. My money must become less. My coat must become less. My time must become less. My own life must become less. The person right in front of me is Jesus, and Jesus must become greater.

What would it be like to live by the mantra of John the Baptist, "He must become greater. I must become less"? When my wife was pregnant with our first child, I gained some sympathy weight. I was also eating for two! I didn't need to gain more weight. Jill needed to gain weight, so I went on a diet and called it the "she-must-become-greater-I-must-become-less diet"!

When people think of you, who is bigger in their minds? Jesus or you?

We've already mentioned Arthur Conan Doyle once. Doyle created a character bigger than himself as a writer. People knew Doyle, but the character he created was so big that he continues in our imaginations today and is recreated over and over in dramas and stories. The character's name, of course, is Sherlock Holmes.

When people think of you, who is bigger in their minds? Jesus or you?

A portion of the "Prayer of St. Patrick" strongly ties to this mantra of John the Baptist and the question, "Who is bigger when people think of you?"

Christ be with me, Christ within me,
Christ behind me, Christ before me,
Christ beside me, Christ to win me,
Christ to comfort me and restore me.
Christ beneath me, Christ above me,
Christ in quiet, Christ in danger,
Christ in hearts of all that love me,
Christ in mouth of friend or stranger.

One version of the prayer says, "Christ in the mouth of everyone who speaks of me." Who is bigger?

The mission team Jill and I served with in Uganda had a mantra first said by mentors at Harding University. "Do something bigger than yourself."

What does it mean to live this mantra in each of our lives? It can permeate every part of our lives and churches. For example, a ministry at our church that does media during our Sunday services has the mantra, "Do not distract with media but point people to God." They want the microphones, sound, projection, video all to work without distracting from the point of it all: Jesus. This team of media volunteers want, as John the Baptist wanted, to point to Jesus. He must become greater. We must become less.

What does it mean for a church as a whole to take on the mantra of John the Baptist? My opinion must become less. My ministry must become less. My preaching must become less. My worship singing or playing must become less. My family, my children, my grandchildren, my job, my reputation, my, my, my . . . must become less, in order for Jesus to become more.

He must become greater. I must become less.

—*Greg*

TRUTH & DARE

DARE THREE

Read John 3:1–36

1. What do you like about this story?

2. What do you not like about this story?

3. What is this story saying to the audience that originally received it and to us today?

4. What is this story calling us to believe?

5. What is this story calling us to do?

6. Are you an undercover follower of Jesus like Nicodemus?

7. What actions, words, attitudes of yours are not obedient to this teaching you've read today?

8. Would you share this story with one person this week?

Jesus and the Samaritan woman at the well.

DARE FOUR:
Worship

*"Most of our troubles stem from our inability
to sit quietly in a room."*
—Blaise Pascal (1623–1662)

IF YOU'RE LIKE US AND YOU GREW UP IN A SMALL
town, then you know that everybody in town saw each other
at the local shopping center. You couldn't avoid somebody
easily, because everybody knew everybody, and everybody
had to go to the local grocery. You saw everybody from work,
from church, from town, because it was the one place where
everyone had to go.

If you visited a small village in Africa, then you would see
the one place where everybody gathers, the one place they have
to go. Where do you think that is? The water source.

In John 4 we have a story about this gathering place where
everybody has to come to get water. But what if you don't want

to see everybody? What if you are an outcast, and you would prefer not to see all those people at the well? That's where this story begins, with Jesus talking to a woman who really doesn't want to be seen by anybody.

We find this to be one of the more moving stories in the book of John. Jesus engages in a serious, profound, theological conversation with somebody who is on the very edges, the margins, of her society. We don't just learn about theology in this story. We learn how to deal with people. For Jesus, there are no people who are outside the possibilities of the Kingdom of God. Whether it's Nicodemus the religious leader, or this woman who's almost ostracized in her world. For Jesus, they all need to hear about the coming of the Kingdom of God. He recognizes this woman's enormous worth and, at the same time, calls her to new life in him. And, in doing this, he sets a model for us about how we engage the world, and in fact, how we engage those on the margins of our world.

The Samaritan woman is the mirror opposite of Nicodemus, Alyce M. McKenzie tells us. "[She] is a living, breathing embodiment of the irony that runs through the Gospel of John: that Jesus was rejected by those we would expect would accept him, and accepted by those we'd expect would reject him."

Nicodemus comes to Jesus at night, and we left him in the twilight between this darkness of misunderstanding Jesus and the light Jesus brings from above. It's obvious when John says, "It was night," that he is envisioning Nicodemus much differently from how he pictures this woman talking to Jesus in daylight at a public place.

We will identify other important contrasts between Nicodemus, an undercover admirer of Jesus, and the Samaritan woman in the reading below. This story found in 4:1–42 is a favorite of many people. It's one of our favorites. As you read, carefully note the contrasts between Nicodemus and the Samaritan woman; watch and listen for images of water and life, and observe how the woman warms to Jesus after an icy first exchange.

> Now Jesus learned that the Pharisees had heard that he was gaining and baptizing more disciples than John— although in fact it was not Jesus who baptized, but his disciples. So he left Judea and went back once more to Galilee.
>
> Now he had to go through Samaria. So he came to a town in Samaria called Sychar, near the plot of ground Jacob had given to his son Joseph. Jacob's well was there, and Jesus, tired as he was from the journey, sat down by the well. It was about noon.
>
> When a Samaritan woman came to draw water, Jesus said to her, "Will you give me a drink?" (His disciples had gone into the town to buy food.)
>
> The Samaritan woman said to him, "You are a Jew and I am a Samaritan woman. How can you ask me for a drink?" (For Jews do not associate with Samaritans.)
>
> Jesus answered her, "If you knew the gift of God and who it is that asks you for a drink, you would have asked him and he would have given you living water."

"Sir," the woman said, "you have nothing to draw with and the well is deep. Where can you get this living water? Are you greater than our father Jacob, who gave us the well and drank from it himself, as did also his sons and his livestock?"

Jesus answered, "Everyone who drinks this water will be thirsty again, but whoever drinks the water I give them will never thirst. Indeed, the water I give them will become in them a spring of water welling up to eternal life."

The woman said to him, "Sir, give me this water so that I won't get thirsty and have to keep coming here to draw water."

He told her, "Go, call your husband and come back."

"I have no husband," she replied.

Jesus said to her, "You are right when you say you have no husband. The fact is, you have had five husbands, and the man you now have is not your husband. What you have just said is quite true."

"Sir," the woman said, "I can see that you are a prophet. Our ancestors worshiped on this mountain, but you Jews claim that the place where we must worship is in Jerusalem."

"Woman," Jesus replied, "believe me, a time is coming when you will worship the Father neither on this mountain nor in Jerusalem. You Samaritans worship what you do not know; we worship what we do know, for salvation is from the Jews. Yet a time is coming and has now come when the true worshipers will worship the Father in the

Spirit and in truth, for they are the kind of worshipers the Father seeks. God is spirit, and his worshipers must worship in the Spirit and in truth."

The woman said, "I know that Messiah" (called Christ) "is coming. When he comes, he will explain everything to us."

Then Jesus declared, "I, the one speaking to you—I am he."

Just then his disciples returned and were surprised to find him talking with a woman. But no one asked, "What do you want?" or "Why are you talking with her?"

Then, leaving her water jar, the woman went back to the town and said to the people, "Come, see a man who told me everything I ever did. Could this be the Messiah?" They came out of the town and made their way toward him.

Meanwhile his disciples urged him, "Rabbi, eat something."

But he said to them, "I have food to eat that you know nothing about."

Then his disciples said to each other, "Could someone have brought him food?"

"My food," said Jesus, "is to do the will of him who sent me and to finish his work. Don't you have a saying, 'It's still four months until harvest'? I tell you, open your eyes and look at the fields! They are ripe for harvest. Even now the one who reaps draws a wage and harvests a crop for eternal life, so that the sower and the reaper may be glad together. Thus the saying 'One sows and

> another reaps' is true. I sent you to reap what you have
> not worked for. Others have done the hard work, and you
> have reaped the benefits of their labor."
>
> Many of the Samaritans from that town believed
> in him because of the woman's testimony, "He told me
> everything I ever did." So when the Samaritans came
> to him, they urged him to stay with them, and he
> stayed two days. And because of his words many more
> became believers.
>
> They said to the woman, "We no longer believe just
> because of what you said; now we have heard for our-
> selves, and we know that this man really is the Savior of
> the world." (4:1–42)

Jesus is breaking several fundamental cultural conventions of his time. He's having a public conversation with a woman. He's having a sophisticated, high-level discussion with a *Samaritan* woman whose past and present are a bit sketchy. In fact, as you were reading, did you notice the disciples' reaction to Jesus talking to the woman?

A group of Christians go out for lunch at a dive that has great food, but it's on the edge of downtown where homeless people hang out. A woman in the parking lot approaches one of the single guys in the group on the way into the restaurant. She doesn't appear homeless but she's at home on the street, and there are some raised eyebrows and shared looks by the women of the group and a few of the men as they go ahead into the restaurant. The single guy talks with the woman for fifteen minutes. Meanwhile, the group orders his usual hamburger for him, and when he arrives at the table, the group all wants to know what the woman wanted and why they talked so long.

Jesus's disciples were curious about what Jesus and this woman could possibly be talking about, and they were put off by the whole thing. Before we judge the disciples, remember that some Christians find it difficult to believe another Christian would have fifteen minutes to wait dinner so he could talk to a homeless person who might be a prostitute or a drug addict.

Doesn't Jesus know what kind of woman this is? Okay, let's just order for him. He always does this! Does he not know she's trying to scam him? Is her game to proposition guys who've obviously been at church? One of the reasons this is a favorite story of ours and of many people is because Jesus goes further than the baseline of treating the woman with respect. He has a conversation with her that would honor any theologian.

Here is the Samaritan woman. She's come to the well to draw out water. Jesus had likely just walked twenty miles since sunrise. It's about noon and likely hot. Jesus is tired and desperately needs water to drink. Could a thirsty Jewish man compromise his values and speak to a woman in public, a Samaritan low-life? Jesus doesn't just open up a forbidden conversation. He asks a very vulnerable and necessary question. He has a legitimate need and asks the woman to fill that need.

"Will you give me a drink?"

The disciples have gone to town to buy food. They are always worried about food. They needn't have been so concerned so much of the time. After all, Jesus could make food!

The Samaritan woman says to Jesus, "You are a Jew and I am a Samaritan woman. How can you ask me for a drink?" John writes a little aside here, one of the many "whispers," as Michael Card calls them, and NIV translators put these whispers in parentheses. It's as if John is narrating a play on stage and, shielding his mouth with the back of his hand, speaks directly to the audience as the actors continue to act as if they are talking. These whispers are also indications of the kind of audience John expects. If he were writing purely to Jews, then the line he whispers here would be unnecessary, so he must assume many non-Jewish readers. His parenthetical statement is this: "For Jews do not associate with Samaritans."

This is a blatant statement of racism. Our twenty-first century sensibilities find racism as off-putting as sexual unfaithfulness, dishonesty, or crime. It's difficult for us to understand the Jew-Samaritan thing, we think. But we all have some kind of latent racism embedded in our hearts. We Americans are only six generations after a war that tore our nation apart. We are only two generations past days when blacks could not even vote. We *are* the generation that has learned to hate a whole new sect of people who attacked our nation on September 11, 2001. Is it really that hard to understand? Or is racism simply difficult to admit?

Could we say flatly that we don't associate with Muslims? We know that would violate our belief in Jesus and his command to associate with all people, to faithfully fulfill the Great Commission to make disciples of all nations. But do many of us have Muslim friends? We could make an analogy for us to understand by pointing to the present day Israeli-Palestinian relationship. Would Jews still say just as plainly, "Jews don't associate with Palestinians"? Would Palestinians say without qualification, "Palestinians don't associate with Jews"?

Racism is subtler today in America. Do you say to a new youth minister at your church, "When you are looking for an apartment, look on this side of town. You won't find anything good on *that side*"? Often, realtors gravitate toward showing properties in certain parts of town for black, white, Asian, Hispanic populations. A raised eyebrow, a clutched purse when passing a person of a different ethnicity may be clues to our racist reactions. Racism can also be patronizing: thinking certain races or immigrants need our assistance, ministry, or outreach, rather than thinking first to—like Jesus—have a conversation with someone unlike us and ask *them* for a cup of water.

So the conversation Jesus enters is tense and off-limits, but Jesus continues to answer the woman's question, "How can you a Jew ask me for water?"

"If you knew the gift of God and who it is that asked you for a drink, you would have asked him and he would have given you living water."

"Sir," the woman says, "you have nothing to draw with and the well is deep. Where can you get this living water? Are you greater than our father Jacob who gave us the well and drank from it himself, as did also his sons and his flocks and his herds?"

In the same way that Nicodemus replies incredulously to what Jesus says, so does the Samaritan woman. She's chippy, even sarcastic. You want to borrow my Nalgene? Who travels without a way to get water? And *you* are promising me sparkling, flowing water?

Keep in mind that the woman is not reading an English translation in a comfy chair with the luxury of understanding symbolically, spiritually, what Jesus may be saying. She's probably thinking about a really good water source Jesus claims to know about.

So she comes back at Jesus. You Jewish men really just always have to outdo each other. Do you think you are better than the one who dug this well, our father Jacob!?

Remember, Jesus is talking from above. People in the stories in John are listening from below.

"Everyone who drinks this water I give them will never thirst again, because this water will become in them a spring of water welling up to eternal life."

The woman says to him—and we think she's still being sarcastic—"Sir, give me this water so I won't get thirsty and have to keep coming here to draw water." This isn't in the text, but what Jesus does again at this point, as with Nicodemus, is roll his eyes.

He told her, "Go, call your husband and come back." Jesus is always doing that, saying stuff that doesn't make sense, throwing up non sequiturs.

"I have no husband," she replies.

Jesus already knows this, of course, so he answers, "You are right when you say you have no husband. The fact is, you've had five husbands and the man you now have is not your husband. What you've said is quite true."

What we immediately assume about the woman here says as much about all of us as it does about her. Do we assume five husbands means she's divorced those men or that she's a home wrecker because the man she has is not her husband and she's having an affair with a married man? That may be the case, but the text does not say all that. She could have lost husbands to abandonment, death, war, or divorce. Still, Jesus must have a reason for pointing out that the one she now is living with is not her husband. The man probably is someone else's husband. And what she'll tell townspeople later, about Jesus knowing "all I ever did" is also an indication that she was convicted of sin in her conversation with Jesus.

"Sir," the woman said, "I can see that you are a prophet." This isn't in the text, but she also implies, ". . . and nosey."

She continues. "Our ancestors worshiped on this mountain, but you Jews claim that the place where we must worship is in Jerusalem."

We need to pause *right there.*

Jesus just has given her the "seer treatment," telling her all about her mottled domestic background. And she responds by asking a theological question! Should you worship in Jerusalem, where the Jews say you ought to worship, or should you worship on Mount Gerizim where the Samaritans say you're supposed to worship? She wants him to straighten out a theological problem that is hundreds of years old.

For years we taught this wrong. The way we used to teach it isn't a bad angle on it: she asks a theological question because she doesn't like the personal turn of the conversation. Jesus is getting too personal, re-opening old wounds, and she changes the subject. Today we often observe people dip into the issue mode when things get too personal. When a conversation gets too personal in a small group or Bible class, suddenly people get incredibly interested in theology.

We're convinced we got this wrong. When Jesus tells her all about her background, she perceives that he's a prophet. She asks him what she believes to be the single most important question in the world. If anything, she's going to the heart of the matter. If this guy can answer *this* question, then he must be the real deal.

> "Woman," Jesus replied, "believe me, a time is coming when you will worship the Father neither on this mountain nor in Jerusalem. You Samaritans worship what you do not know; we worship what we do know, for salvation is from the Jews. Yet a time is coming and has now come when the true worshipers will worship the Father in the Spirit and in truth, for they are the kind of worshipers the Father seeks. God is spirit, and his worshipers must worship in the Spirit and in truth."
>
> The woman said, "I know that Messiah (called Christ) is coming. When he comes, he will explain everything to us."
>
> Then Jesus declared, "I, the one speaking to you—I am he." (4:21–26)

She's asked a theological question: Do the Jews have it right, or do the Samaritans have it right? Jesus basically says, I have to level with you, the Jews have it right and the Samaritans have it wrong. It's not on Mount Gerizim. It's in Jerusalem, and in fact salvation comes through the Jews. Then he says something more. By the way, he tells her, none of this matters anymore. This new age is coming and now is.

Now we have to pause again to preach a mini-sermon ... about football. The time is coming and now has come. Long time ago, there was a football coach who was extremely successful but was impossible to get along with. We might think of him as the Bill Belichick of his time. His name was George Allen. He coached what was then the Los Angeles Rams. Even though he was an excellent coach, he couldn't get along with anyone, so they fired him.

Allen was then hired by a team that had been monumentally awful at the time, the Washington Redskins. They had a team, but it was debatable whether they could call it a professional team. They hired George Allen, who decided he wanted to win because he hated so badly to lose. He came up with a strategy not to build over several years but to win now. He traded away all their future draft choices and instead acquired a bunch of players who were Hall of Fame caliber but were nearly too old for football. They were called the over-the-hill gang.

The over-the-hill gang took George Allen's Redskins to the Super Bowl. They lost the big game, but getting there was a monumental achievement. This team had a slogan. The slogan was, "The future is now." The reality was, it had better be now, because they had no future! They had traded their future away.

Think about this idea when you think about John. The future is now. The future has already come into the present, so the new order is neither Jerusalem nor Gerizim as the center of worship. That time has already come. The center of worship is no longer a place. The center of worship is a person. It's not about Jerusalem. It's not about Gerizim. It's about Jesus. Because of the very nature of God, if you're going to worship God, you have to do it spiritually and truly. Those are adverbs, by the way, in the original text. What does that mean? It means you have to worship spiritually and truly through Jesus. The center of worship is not a place, it's not a time. It's a person. It's Jesus.

The story of the Samaritan woman is so much more than we originally thought, probably more than you've ever thought it was. The story of the Samaritan woman is one of the most important texts on worship to be found in the Bible. We get confused about worship. We tend to think that worship is about getting all of the forms correct, but Jesus says what it's about is getting the Messiah correct. The story has this nice little ending. The disciples show up just in time to do nothing. They return, are surprised to find their Rabbi talking with a woman, but no one asks, What do you want? or Why are you talking with her?

Then the woman scurries away and leaves her water jar. She goes back to the town and says to the people, "Come, see a man who told me everything I ever did. Could this be the Messiah?"

What the woman asks is the big question in John. In John 3, we have Jesus talking to the most Jewish guy of all Jewish guys, Nicodemus. Here we have him talking to this immoral Samaritan woman. The message, however, is the same. There's one way to God, says Jesus: through me. You want to know about true worship? True worship has to do with knowing

God, and you know God insofar as you know Jesus. Worship is always about a person.

We take risks when we gather for worship, because we all have secrets, just as the Samaritan woman had secrets. Many of these secrets are quite painful. When our secrets are revealed as Jesus reveals the secrets of the woman, we may feel ashamed or fear that we might lose our reputation. We may be afraid that people will walk away from us, stop liking us, stop asking for our opinion, stop respecting us, or worst of all, un-friend us on Facebook.

But Jesus is a secret-revealer of God—a necessary part of discipleship. Secrets keep disciples in the dark. Light, water, bread, wine, and then blood, sweat, and tears are the stuff that flows in and out of the pores, nostrils, and mouths of disciples of Jesus. Secrets are obstacles of belief, and Jesus wants to reveal not just a hunky-dory buddyship we can have with him, but one that x-rays us or gives our brains and hearts an MRI. Our hearts are revealed in the presence of Jesus. We ask theoretical questions like Nicodemus, theological questions like the Samaritan woman, and Jesus comes back with, "Go, get your husband," or "You are a big shot leader and you don't know this?"

If we walk or run away from Jesus, sure of ourselves, *not* scratching our heads like Nicodemus, *not* running back to town to tell someone, are we any better than they? Confession is living water; Christ is present and revealing God when we confess our sins to one another and to God.

TRUTH & DARE

DARE FOUR

Reminder: There is no special dare beyond reading and acting on these questions. This is the way to daring faith. Read John 4:1–42

1. What do you like about this story?

2. What do you not like about this story?

3. What is this story saying to the audience that originally received it and to us today?

4. What is this story calling us to believe?

5. What is this story calling us to do?

6. What actions, words, attitudes of yours are not obedient to this teaching you've read today?

7. Would you share this story with one person this week?

DARE FIVE:
Christian Cannibalism

"Cannibals don't eat clowns, because they taste funny."
—Unknown, because no one wants to claim this bad joke

UNIVERSITY CAFETERIAS HAVE CHANGED A LOT from what they were when we went to school. We had few choices. But now there are all sorts of serving lines. You can have hamburgers, pizza, pasta, Cajun food! There's nearly every choice you'd want to eat: meat lover's pizza, vegetarian dishes, gluten free. But there's one serving line you'll never find out there. There is no serving line labeled, "Human Flesh." We don't have a line for cannibals. We accommodate everyone else's taste, but not cannibals.

One of the very few stories told in all four Gospels is about a meal where there is no choice in food selection. You get fish and bread. No other choices. And it turns into an amazing sermon about, of all things, cannibalism. At least, that's what it sounds like.

What does the story of Jesus multiplying bread and fish tell us about God? We know what it says about humans: we love to eat for free! When John tells the story, though, he puts a strange twist on it.

> Some time after this, Jesus crossed to the far shore of the Sea of Galilee (that is, the Sea of Tiberias), and a great crowd of people followed him because they saw the signs he had performed by healing the sick. Then Jesus went up on a mountainside and sat down with his disciples. The Jewish Passover Festival was near.
>
> When Jesus looked up and saw a great crowd coming toward him, he said to Philip, "Where shall we buy bread for these people to eat?" He asked this only to test him, for he already had in mind what he was going to do. (6:1–6)

Whenever Jesus asks a question in John, it's never to get information. It's a test.

> Philip answered him, "It would take more than half a year's wages to buy enough bread for each one to have a bite!"
>
> Another of his disciples, Andrew, Simon Peter's brother, spoke up, "Here is a boy with five small barley loaves and two small fish, but how far will they go among so many?" (6:7–9)

Andrew brings the boy to Jesus. No small thing. It may be that the best thing we could ever do in our lives is to be known as someone who brings people to Jesus.

> Jesus said, "Have the people sit down." There was plenty of grass in that place, and they sat down (about five thousand men were there). Jesus then took the loaves, gave thanks, and distributed to those who were seated as much as they wanted. He did the same with the fish.
>
> When they had all had enough to eat, he said to his disciples, "Gather the pieces that are left over. Let nothing be wasted." So they gathered them and filled twelve baskets with the pieces of the five barley loaves left over by those who had eaten.
>
> After the people saw the sign Jesus performed, they began to say, "Surely this is the Prophet who is to come into the world." Jesus, knowing that they intended to come and make him king by force, withdrew again to a mountain by himself. (6:10–15)

What got your attention in the story? A couple of things in the way John tells the story caught our attention. First, he says there were five thousand men in the desert. Five thousand men in a deserted place doing what? Just to listen to a speech? Some Bible scholars have speculated that this was a paramilitary gathering. They looked at Jesus and said this looks like the guy we've been waiting for, and they followed him out into the desert, and so in the minds of many who gathered there that day, this was the beginning of a new revolt against Roman occupation.

Whatever the purpose of this gathering was, Jesus fed them. And after they were fed, they approached him to make him king. Sounds like an army, or at least a politically motivated group. We wondered when we read the story of Nicodemus if he wasn't part of an exploratory committee looking for a charismatic rabbi who could re-ignite Jewish preeminence in Zion. Could this seaside dinner-on-the-ground have been a further extension of those political dreams?

Think about the qualifications Jesus had to lead a military and political revolution. He could heal the sick, raise the dead, and multiply food. That pretty much took care of most military logistic and tactical problems. This was their guy. He was the one they had been waiting for, and they were going to make him king. By force.

This idea of "making him king" is peculiar to us. How often do we pick someone up on our shoulders and make him king? We're more likely to squash our politicians, cut them down to size, or worse, ignore them in order to prove they can't truly rule over us. We think of kings as fat throne sitters who will squeeze the guilders out of us. In many countries, including the United States, we have a much different mentality about politics than did the fish-eaters who were trying to make Jesus king. They wanted a king who ruled benevolently. While they were living in a different political system than we do, their response to the government was the same then as now: fewer taxes, better roads, and more food.

This crowd thought Jesus was more than a great teacher. By his miracles, he was more. He will be our king! But this never happened. They didn't make him king. Neither we readers of this Gospel nor the people in this story knew where Jesus went. He slipped away.

We're going to skip the big scene of Jesus walking on the water, in order to more closely connect Jesus's feeding the multitudes with his teaching about bread. If we were writing a movie script, we'd definitely spend time watching Jesus walk on water, but we can't do the scene justice here if we stay focused on food. The next day a bunch of the folks who gobbled up Jesus's free food on the other side of the lake the day before showed up again at dinner time. Guess what they wanted?

When they found him on the other side of the lake, they asked him, "Rabbi, when did you get here?"

Jesus answered, "Very truly I tell you, you are looking for me, not because you saw the signs I performed but because you ate the loaves and had your fill. Do not work for food that spoils, but for food that endures to eternal life, which the Son of Man will give you. For on him God the Father has placed his seal of approval."

Then they asked him, "What must we do to do the works God requires?"

Jesus answered, "The work of God is this: to believe in the one he has sent."

So they asked him, "What sign then will you give that we may see it and believe you? What will you do? Our ancestors ate the manna in the wilderness; as it is written: 'He gave them bread from heaven to eat.'"

Jesus said to them, "Very truly I tell you, it is not Moses who has given you the bread from heaven, but it

> is my Father who gives you the true bread from heaven.
> For the bread of God is the bread that comes down from
> heaven and gives life to the world."
>
> "Sir," they said, "always give us this bread." (6:25–34)

Jesus kept re-directing their human desire from food that spoils to eternal bread that comes down from heaven and gives life to the world. He warned against working for food that spoils and instead urges them to do the "work of God," which he said is "to believe in the one he has sent."

Would you please issue us a "pun-pass" here? The feeding of the multitude is a great story in itself, but John is baking up something we don't smell in the other Gospels. Here Jesus went one step further with the idea that God feeds his people. Now he said, "I am the one who feeds you my own flesh and blood."

> Then Jesus declared, "I am the bread of life. Whoever
> comes to me will never go hungry, and whoever believes
> in me will never be thirsty. But as I told you, you have
> seen me and still you do not believe. All those the Father
> gives me will come to me, and whoever comes to me I
> will never drive away. For I have come down from heaven
> not to do my will but to do the will of him who sent me.
> And this is the will of him who sent me, that I shall lose
> none of all those he has given me, but raise them up at
> the last day. For my Father's will is that everyone who
> looks to the Son and believes in him shall have eternal
> life, and I will raise them up at the last day."
>
> At this the Jews there began to grumble about him
> because he said, "I am the bread that came down from

heaven." They said, "Is this not Jesus, the son of Joseph, whose father and mother we know? How can he now say, 'I came down from heaven'?"

"Stop grumbling among yourselves," Jesus answered. "No one can come to me unless the Father who sent me draws them, and I will raise them up at the last day. It is written in the Prophets: 'They will all be taught by God.' Everyone who has heard the Father and learned from him comes to me. No one has seen the Father except the one who is from God; only he has seen the Father. Very truly I tell you, the one who believes has eternal life. I am the bread of life. Your ancestors ate the manna in the wilderness, yet they died. But here is the bread that comes down from heaven, which anyone may eat and not die. I am the living bread that came down from heaven. Whoever eats this bread will live forever. This bread is my flesh, which I will give for the life of the world."

Then the Jews began to argue sharply among themselves, "How can this man give us his flesh to eat?"

Jesus said to them, "Very truly I tell you, unless you eat the flesh of the Son of Man and drink his blood, you have no life in you. Whoever eats my flesh and drinks my blood has eternal life, and I will raise them up at the last day. For my flesh is real food and my blood is real drink. Whoever eats my flesh and drinks my blood remains in me, and I in them. Just as the living Father sent me and I live because of the Father, so the one who feeds on me will live because of me. This is the bread that came down from heaven. Your ancestors ate manna and died, but

> whoever feeds on this bread will live forever." He said this while teaching in the synagogue in Capernaum.
>
> On hearing it, many of his disciples said, "This is a hard teaching. Who can accept it?" (6:35–60)

After he fed the five thousand, Jesus's popularity rating was helium—one hundred percent. The next day he told them the true meaning of this feeding. "I am the bread of life." Now they were confused and his approval rating started to slip. Then he told them this bread was his own body. His approval rating plunged to an all-time low. Finally, he claimed a direct connection to the Father. And, as one last bonus, he claimed that he was edible.

Loosely translated, many of Jesus's erstwhile disciples say, "Whoa, this is a hard teaching. Anyone here able to move forward with this guy we wanted to make king yesterday?"

> Aware that his disciples were grumbling about this, Jesus said to them, "Does this offend you? Then what if you see the Son of Man ascend to where he was before! The Spirit gives life; the flesh counts for nothing. The words I have spoken to you—they are full of the Spirit and life. Yet there are some of you who do not believe." For Jesus had known from the beginning which of them did not believe and who would betray him. He went on to say, "This is why I told you that no one can come to me unless the Father has enabled them."
>
> From this time many of his disciples turned back and no longer followed him.

"You do not want to leave too, do you?" Jesus asked
the Twelve.

Simon Peter answered him, "Lord, to whom shall we
go? You have the words of eternal life. We have come to
believe and to know that you are the Holy One of God."

Then Jesus replied, "Have I not chosen you, the
Twelve? Yet one of you is a devil!" (He meant Judas, the
son of Simon Iscariot, who, though one of the Twelve,
was later to betray him.) (6:61–71)

When Christians today hear "eat my flesh and drink my blood,"
we normally think of the Lord's Supper, but Jesus was probably
talking about something else as well. Since the Lord's Supper is
very important, you can read more by our friend, John Mark
Hicks, in his book *Come to the Table*. But we want to focus on
something else Jesus seems to be saying here.

When Jesus said, "You have to eat my flesh and drink
my blood," many of his followers responded, "How can this
man give us his flesh to eat?" Their gut reaction was how we
would respond if we thought someone was talking literally
about eating his flesh. In Africa when we read this text, people
reacted the same way we do in the United States: "Eeew." That
was the reaction of the Jews in the story as well: "Eeew." How
can he give us his flesh to eat? Did he *really* just say that?

The greatest uninspired commentary on this story and on
Jesus's words about eating his flesh and drinking his blood may
be one based on a true story of a rugby team who survived
a plane crash high in the Andes Mountains. On their way to
play a match, the rugby team was flying over the mountains

when their plane went down. The story is dramatized in the 1993 movie, *ALIVE,* directed by Frank Marshall and starring Ethan Hawke, Vincent Spano, and Josh Hamilton.

When they crashed in the Andes, some were killed. Some survived.

That began one of the great survival stories of the modern age. Here they were, stuck high in the Andes. How were they going to survive? No rescue attempt could reasonably be attempted until spring. One thing we admire about athletes is their heart, their desire to win. And the converse is also part of their passion. They hate to lose.

We know what we would do in this terrible situation. We'd curl up in a ball and prepare to die. But not these guys. They start to solve their problems. The broken fuselage of their plane became their shelter. They melted snow for water, but they had a serious problem. They had no food. The plane was carrying little food, and you can't live on peanuts all winter.

They had a conversation we know little about because those who could tell about it are understandably tight-lipped. Somebody in the group said, "We have food here. We have frozen meat. If you're willing to step across the most difficult of human taboos and eat human flesh, we can survive."

They had a discussion and they decided to do it. We have to be careful with this story at this point because we want to honor the kind of decision they made. This is going to sound cuter than we want it to: It's one thing to eat a stranger. It's another thing to eat a teammate and a friend.

Someone had to take a knife and go to their dead, frozen teammates who did not survive the crash, and . . . you can imagine the rest. And so they did. They cannibalized their dead teammates, and they survived. That is not the end of the story, however, because the question is now this: We *survived,* but how do we now *live* with this the rest of our lives?

You face the parents of those who died and they say, "Where are the bodies?"

"There are no bodies."

"Why?"

"We ate them."

Then there is that one parent who sees it so clearly and says, "I can imagine my son would have chosen no greater way to die than to be a source of life for his friends." And that parent could have been quoting directly from the words of Jesus found in John 15:13, "Greater love has no one than this, that he lay down his life for his friends."

Then the irony of the situation hits us. If everyone had survived the plane crash, everyone would have died. Because some died and became food for their teammates, some survived.

Now back to the story of Jesus feeding the multitudes not bread and fish alone, but himself. How can this man give us his flesh to eat? We know the question and the answer. He is going to freely decide to lay down his life to become the source of life for us. You have to appreciate the great irony of this story. They had just tried to make him king. Jesus's response was not to accept the kingship but instead to offer himself as food that gives life.

I'm not going to be king; I'm going to be food for the world.

Later in the book of John we'll see Jesus develop this idea of not being just the Son of God, but also being the One who lays down his life to become the source of life for us. In this story of Christian cannibalism, Jesus refuses military rule. He refuses to be their king. He instead becomes food. That's what we learn about God in this story. God is food for us. As our friend, Mark Moore, says in his book, God longs to nourish us with himself.

To be followers of Jesus, we follow the One who says, If you're going to follow me, I'm not going to be the kind of king or general you want me to be. Instead, I'm going to be the One who lays down his life so that you will be able to eat and live.

Every Sunday Christians from all over the world sit together and, in the words of Jesus, "eat my flesh and drink my blood." This has become a powerful symbol for Christians, reminding believers that the continuing presence of Christ together with them is crucial to life. In this story Jesus depicts himself less as mighty Lord and more as simple nourishing food for hungry people coming to his table looking for life.

Jesus claims to be not the world's most powerful man but simple food for those who want to live.

Andrew: Bringing People to Jesus

Read John 1:35–51; 6:1–9; 12:20–26. Pay attention to what Andrew does. It's no small thing but it barely receives notice in the synoptic Gospels, and if we're not aware, we may also miss it in John.

What he does may be one of the best things any of us could ever do. This thing we like about Andrew,

Simon Peter's brother, seems a small thing, but it was huge then and still is for us today. Andrew in the book of John is intentionally shown bringing people to Jesus.

We use this phrase today when we speak of evangelism, so when someone becomes a disciple of Christ, we say the person who shared the gospel "brought them to Jesus." Whether or not this language comes from what Andrew does, we don't know. But Andrew literally brings people face to face to meet Jesus. You can see in the readings mentioned above, that after spending time with Jesus, Andrew finds his brother Peter and says, "We have found the Messiah!" and he takes him to Jesus.

Can we even imagine the gospel story, the early church, important writings of the church, and early leadership without Peter in the picture? Andrew does no small thing to bring his brother to Jesus. In the readings you'll also see Andrew bringing a boy with food to Jesus, and Jesus multiplies the food to feed thousands of people. Later, when Philip doesn't seem to know what to do with some Greeks who want to see Jesus, he tells Andrew, and Andrew does know what to do.

He brings the Greeks to Jesus.

—Greg

TRUTH & DARE

DARE FIVE

Read John 6:1–71

1. What do you like about this story?

2. What do you not like about this story?

3. What is this story saying to the audience that originally received it?

4. What is this story calling us to believe?

5. What is this story calling us to do?

6. What actions, words, attitudes of yours are not obedient to this teaching you've read today?

7. Would you share this Jesus story with one person this week?

DARE SIX:
I Was Blind but Now I See

"God is a great humorist, but he has a slow audience."
—Garrison Keillor

CAN YOU IMAGINE GETTING EXPELLED FROM YOUR church? The very idea that you could be kicked out of your church is a devastating thought. This would wreck everything for you. These are the same people you do life with. You'd have to pick up stakes and leave town. You could barely function.

While not everyone would agree, we think John 9 is the center of John's book. The single most important episode in John is the story of the blind man. At this center in John 9, we learn what the writer is really up to in his Gospel. The story is beautifully told of Jesus healing a man who was blind since birth. While the story is central in John, ironically the blind man is not the true focus of the story. Ah, you are ahead of us.

Jesus is always the main character. True, but that's not what we meant. Watch for two other people in the story who are the focal point. Both the blind man and these two others in the story are faced with that same alarming idea that they might do something that would get them kicked out of their synagogue, which for them would be very much like getting kicked out of your hometown church and community. It is this moment in John when we come face to face with daring faith.

> As he went along, he saw a man blind from birth. His disciples asked him, "Rabbi, who sinned, this man or his parents, that he was born blind?" (9:1)

Did you notice the disciples' question? It's a question about Deuteronomic theology. Deuteronomic theology means you can tell about a person's spiritual condition by looking at their physical condition. Since Yogi Berra died during the writing of this book, we can honor the baseball player and man of words with one of his quotes that describes the thinking of Deuteronomic theology. Yogi said, "You can observe a lot by just watching."

So Deuteronomic theology says, If you see a person who is healthy and wealthy, God really loves them; if you see somebody who is poor or unhealthy, that means God has placed a curse on them.

Jesus's disciples are asking him to apply Deuteronomic theology with the blind man as the lab rat. When they see this person who is born blind, they think somebody must have really made God mad. They want to know, Who's the guilty one here? He was born blind. So it must be either his own sin that caused blindness or his parents' sin.

Of course, we're interested to know how Jesus answers the disciples' question. Because pieces of Deuteronomic theology linger in our minds. Did I do something to deserve this? Is God punishing me? I have terrible luck. Am I sure it's really luck? Maybe it's all choices and God is not really involved. Could God at least be chastening me so I'll pay attention? Doesn't God even punish whole nations for sin and rebellion against him?

Yes, we're interested in this important issue, as the disciples were. So, enter the moment with the disciples, standing and looking at the blind man just as you might see a homeless man with a cardboard sign that says, "Veteran. Will work for food. Anything helps." Did our nation cause this? Are we cursed? Who sinned? Am I part of this? Do I get involved?

Yes, we're interested in Jesus's response to the disciples' question, because it is still the question of the day. Could we suspend judgment of the disciples and forgive them for their bluntness in asking Jesus the question? Why don't we ask Jesus the same question about all our similar dilemmas? Maybe in this story we can find our answer.

Maybe, but the answer doesn't come the way the disciples or we might expect. Jesus answers the multiple-choice quiz the disciples give him. They give him an A-or-B test question, and Jesus responds with an essay answer. We often give God such limited boxes to check. We try to find reasons people are suffering. For example, we might think people in "bad neighborhoods" did something to deserve living there. We might conversely think if we live in a so-called "good neigh-borhood" that we did something to deserve it. Who sinned? Who deserves this curse or blessing?

Jesus upends this kind of thinking just as he upset the tables in the Temple courts. Jesus says, "Neither." That one word rocks the foundations of our moral world that we want to control with explanations about why some people have and others have not, some people suffer and others do not.

> "Neither this man nor his parents sinned," said Jesus, "but this happened so that the works of God might be displayed in him. As long as it is day, we must do the works of him who sent me. Night is coming, when no one can work. While I am in the world, I am the light of the world." (9:3–5)

Jesus says, "Neither," and it upsets our multiple-choice world. Then he heals the man born blind.

> After saying this, he spit on the ground, made some mud with the saliva, and put it on the man's eyes. "Go," he told him, "wash in the Pool of Siloam" (this word means "Sent"). So the man went and washed, and came home seeing.
>
> His neighbors and those who had formerly seen him begging asked, "Isn't this the same man who used to sit and beg?" Some claimed that he was.
>
> Others said, "No, he only looks like him."
>
> But he himself insisted, "I am the man." (9:6–9)

This is funny to us that he keeps insisting, "I'm the guy!" The man, formerly known as the blind man, has a new set of problems now that he has sight. As the story progresses, he has not seen the end of his new problems.

"How then were your eyes opened?" they asked.

He replied, "The man they call Jesus made some mud and put it on my eyes. He told me to go to Siloam and wash. So I went and washed, and then I could see."

"Where is this man?" they asked him.

"I don't know," he said.

They brought to the Pharisees the man who had been blind. Now the day on which Jesus had made the mud and opened the man's eyes was a Sabbath. Therefore the Pharisees also asked him how he had received his sight. "He put mud on my eyes," the man replied, "and I washed, and now I see."

Some of the Pharisees said, "This man is not from God, for he does not keep the Sabbath." (9:10–16)

A belief among the Jews at that time was that if every Jew kept the Sabbath perfectly just one time, the end of the world would come. The Kingdom of God would be set in motion. When you see all these arguments about Sabbath, keep this in mind. It's important to them, and it's not something for us to laugh off as if they were totally, well, blind. Actually, that's part of what John is trying to show us: blind people see and people who think they see are blind. Deuteronomic Yogi Berra has no corner on the market of observation, so watch carefully what comes next.

But others asked, "How can a sinner perform such signs?" So they were divided.

Then they turned again to the blind man, "What have you to say about him? It was your eyes he opened."

The man replied, "He is a prophet."

They still did not believe that he had been blind and had received his sight until they sent for the man's parents. "Is this your son?" they asked. "Is this the one you say was born blind? How is it that now he can see?"

"We know he is our son," the parents answered, "and we know he was born blind. But how he can see now, or who opened his eyes, we don't know. Ask him. He is of age; he will speak for himself." His parents said this because they were afraid of the Jewish leaders, who already had decided that anyone who acknowledged that Jesus was the Messiah would be put out of the synagogue. That was why his parents said, "He is of age; ask him."

A second time they summoned the man who had been blind. "Give glory to God by telling the truth," they said. "We know this man is a sinner."

He replied, "Whether he is a sinner or not, I don't know. One thing I do know. I was blind but now I see!"

Then they asked him, "What did he do to you? How did he open your eyes?"

He answered, "I have told you already and you did not listen. Why do you want to hear it again? Do you want to become his disciples too?"

Then they hurled insults at him and said, "You are this fellow's disciple! We are disciples of Moses! We know that God spoke to Moses, but as for this fellow, we don't even know where he comes from."

The man answered, "Now that is remarkable! You don't know where he comes from, yet he opened my eyes.

> We know that God does not listen to sinners. He listens
> to the godly person who does his will. Nobody has ever
> heard of opening the eyes of a man born blind. If this
> man were not from God, he could do nothing."
>
> To this they replied, "You were steeped in sin at
> birth; how dare you lecture us!" And they threw him out.
> (9:16b–34)

They throw the blind man out of the synagogue, and the text doesn't say this next part, but it could be added, because the religious leaders are losing the argument.

Here's the story summarized so far. Here's a guy who was born blind. The disciples think someone sinned, but Jesus says that's not the case. This happened so God's deeds may be seen in this man. Then Jesus heals him. The Pharisees say we don't know where this Jesus comes from. They ask the blind man, "How do you think he healed you?" The formerly blind man says, "I don't know. I just know one thing. I was blind, but now I see."

The formerly blind man does a very important thing here: he sees and bears witness to what Jesus did.

Those of us who preach often are frustrated when we go out of town and they put up some person in the church to preach in our place. The person doesn't know biblical languages or theology. And because they don't know what else to do, they simply tell it like they see it, bear witness to what God has done in their lives. Then the preacher comes back from his vacation and finds out everybody likes that "preacher" better. Believe us, in our preaching careers, we've had this experience a time or two! But we've learned to smile and remember what's happening here: a disciple got in front of the body of Christ and bore witness to what God is doing today, just like the blind man did.

I don't know about this man's doctrines, but I know I'm the guy who was blind, regardless of what the neighbors tell you. I was blind, but now I see.

The blind man is bearing witness. I was blind, but now I see.

Remember we said this story is not primarily about the blind man? It's also not about the Pharisees. The stories are always and ever *about* Jesus, but the central tension in this story is in the response of the parents of the blind man. The story hinges on the parents *not* bearing witness, not daring faith.

The parents, of course, admit that the blind man is their son. And they can't imagine he's been faking blindness all these years, maybe so that he can have this moment where he tricks everyone!? But when it comes to giving credit to the One who did this miracle, they come up short. Why? They are afraid. What are they afraid of? Their son whom they nursed blind, and taught to walk blind, to eat without making a huge mess, to take care of personal hygiene and use the toilet without sight has now received sight for the first time in his life. They'd never seen the look of recognition in his eyes. After his healing, in a crowded place, it may have been necessary for them to tell their adult son that they are his parents. He's never seen their faces.

John takes pains to explain why the parents are afraid. They are afraid of getting kicked out of the synagogue. As we saw earlier in the book, this fear in John's audience of getting kicked out of their synagogues is probably one big reason he's written his Gospel story. Christians are starting to get kicked out of the synagogues because it's becoming clear they aren't really a different sort of Jew, but something else entirely.

One more important part of the story remains for us to read, then we'll wrap up. In this last segment of the story, Jesus explains that the blind man is the one who really sees, who dares faith. The parents and the religious rulers who claim they can see are really blind.

> Jesus heard that they had thrown him out, and when he found him, he said, "Do you believe in the Son of Man?"
>
> "Who is he, sir?" the man asked. "Tell me so that I may believe in him."
>
> Jesus said, "You have now seen him; in fact, he is the one speaking with you."
>
> Then the man said, "Lord, I believe," and he worshiped him.
>
> Jesus said, "For judgment I have come into this world, so that the blind will see and those who see will become blind."
>
> Some Pharisees who were with him heard him say this and asked, "What? Are we blind too?"
>
> Jesus said, "If you were blind, you would not be guilty of sin; but now that you claim you can see, your guilt remains." (9:35–41)

This is where our approach differs a bit from Christian inspiration books. We might spend some time here talking about the flowers, the intricate wings of a fly the blind man can now see. Things he could only touch and hear buzzing in his ear before all this happened. His mother's voice naturally matches the face of that woman standing over there crying now. But we're more apt to say something like this: Now that the blind man has his sight, his problems are only beginning. Immediately after the healing, Jesus is nowhere to be found. The blind man is on his own. Even his parents do not stand with him in celebrating his sight.

In John's story the parents seem weak. They seem opposed to God and their son. They seem more worried about their social position than about their son or the Messiah. It's as if John is writing to his readers to say, "Is getting kicked out of the synagogue really that awful?" He wants his readers to see themselves in the parents of the blind man. Wouldn't it be worth getting kicked out of the synagogue to confess the truth that God healed your son?

Now we come to an important concept in John. Miracles are only *signs* to people who are ready to see them. It's actually possible for a miracle *not* to be a sign. Some people see a man receive sight, but they are blind to the sign. They are the blind ones, as Jesus points out to the religious leaders at the end of the story.

Those who see the sign clearly, see it as a sign that Jesus is the Messiah. Namely, the blind man sees, and he confesses that Jesus is the Messiah. Then the story becomes a sign to us. In John there are people all over the place who see miracles but never truly see Jesus. This is another story about Jesus, the Messiah, and about seeing him. All the stories in John are about seeing the Messiah, eating the food the Messiah gives, believing in the life he brings.

It seems many people both in Jesus's time and today would rather have miracles than a Messiah. Other Christians die for their belief in Jesus. If you don't believe us, go to www.persecution.com; Voice of the Martyrs exists to support and encourage those being persecuted all over the world because of their public, daring faith in the Messiah. A time may come when you will be called upon to pay the price for following Jesus. Is getting kicked out of the synagogue really so bad when you have a Savior who can give sight to a person born blind?

To the first readers of John who had the same thing at stake as the blind man and his parents, this story was not just literary gold. It was a story that caused them to take a risk and follow Jesus, regardless of the consequences. They would have rightly seen this story as a cautionary tale about people who do not dare believe and bear witness to the Messiah. And the question comes to us as well today. Are we, are you, willing to risk your reputation, your job, your family, your health, your security, your citizenship, your retirement, your long life, for a life of following Jesus?

TRUTH & DARE

DARE SIX

Read John 9:1–41

1. What does Jesus say when the disciples ask whose fault it is that the man was born blind?

2. Does his answer match up with Christian explanations today?

3. How is God's work seen in the man? Only in the miracle, in his faith, or in something else?

4. What do you dislike and like about the story of the blind man?

5. What specific action or inaction does God seem to want from you, from others, from the church?

6. What actions, words, attitudes of yours are not obedient to this teaching you've read today?

7. Who is a person with whom God wants you to share what you've learned from the Gospel of John this week?

DARE SEVEN:
Raising the Rotting Dead

"Faith is not assent to a series of faith statements but assent to the truth of Jesus' relationship with God and the decisive change that relationship means for the lives of those who believe."
—Gail O'Day

AS MINISTERS, WE'VE SPENT OUR SHARE OF TIME in funeral homes. Many of you have been there too, saying that final goodbye to a person you care about. You feel numbness, shock. With tears you feel the finality of never seeing your loved one again in this life. The very faint sense that this finality could ever be reversed is what makes the story told in John 11 so astounding.

A man is dead four days, and Jesus raises him from the dead. Almost everybody agrees that the greatest miracle Jesus ever did was the raising of Lazarus. The miracle is a sign foreshadowing Jesus's own resurrection from death.

The story is remarkably short. There are so many things we'd like to know, but the details aren't there. What's it like to be dead? How does the family really react when the person they said goodbye to comes back from death? What do they talk about after he is raised? While the story doesn't tell us these things, one thing is clear: Jesus is the source of new life.

Of all the "I Am" sayings in John, "I am the resurrection and the life" is the most compelling to us. We have our problems believing, not just in theory, but also in reality. When we're in a funeral home, it's hard for us to think about the promise we have of new life in Christ. And a part of us probably wishes for this kind of rising of Lazarus in the here and now, but the promise of this Gospel story is clear. What God has started, he will finish in Jesus Christ. "I am the resurrection and the life" is true not for Lazarus alone. Jesus promises there is always new life for those who follow him.

Healing the sick is good. But Jesus goes from good to great when he raises the dead. Even to us today, raising dead bodies when they are rotting is truly spectacular.

The key character in the raising of Lazarus is actually one you hardly notice. Of course the story bears his name, but it's somewhat difficult for the dead body of Lazarus to have lines. Even after he is raised, Lazarus doesn't speak.

The main character in the Lazarus story is one of his sisters. The whole story revolves around the reaction of Martha, a hinge in the story John is telling, where some of Jesus's followers must make a choice: believe his radical claims or reject them. In one of the most pivotal scenes in John, Martha declares the deepest truth, at precisely the moment when her heart is broken and she is most disappointed in Jesus. Martha gets a bad rap, because we teach only (and over and over) about the time when she griped to Jesus about how Mary was not helping in the kitchen. But she is the star in John. Martha makes a daring faith declaration that in other Gospels comes out of the mouth of Peter. Her declaration is vital to Christian witness for all time.

As ministers, we often scramble to see a dying church member *before* they die. In the Lazarus story, Jesus takes pains to see Lazarus *after* he dies. Not only that, but Jesus also fiddles around long enough to make sure the corpse is plenty dead before he goes to Bethany, where Lazarus has been interred in a tomb. It's now several days after Lazarus died, and Jesus goes to greet the grieving sisters. His apostles go with him even though they're not crazy about the idea. A travel advisory had been put out: anyone caught with this so-called Messiah is *persona non grata*. He could get exactly what they're plotting for Jesus.

Upon his arrival at the tomb, Jesus finds Lazarus has already been in the tomb four days. Bethany is less than two miles from Jerusalem, and many Jews have come to comfort Martha and Mary in the loss of their brother. When Martha hears that Jesus is coming, she goes out to meet him, but Mary stays at home.

"Lord," Martha says to Jesus, "if you had been here, my brother would not have died, but I know that even now God will give you whatever you ask."

Jesus says to her, "Your brother will rise again."

Martha answers, "I know he will rise again in the resurrection at the last day."

Once again, Jesus is having a theological conversation with a woman. Martha expresses her beliefs in the form of a disappointed scolding of Jesus: "If you had been here, my brother wouldn't have died."

When Martha speaks about the resurrection on the last day, she is expressing the Pharisees' theological position: there will be a resurrection in the end times. The Sadducees believed in no such resurrection. They were sad, you see. Sorry, did we already use that "pun-pass"? Yes, but we know we haven't used the "very tired *old* pun-pass," so . . . anyway, we're going to side with the Pharisees, but that's not what Jesus is talking about when he speaks of resurrection.

> Jesus said to her, "I am the resurrection and the life. The one who believes in me will live, even though they die; and whoever lives by believing in me will never die. Do you believe this?" (11:25–26)

Faith is not something you have. Faith is something you do. Remember, earlier in the book we said the noun form for *faith*, in Greek, does not occur in John? If you read our English translation with *faith* as a verb, here is how it reads.

> Jesus said to her, "I am the resurrection and the life. The one who faiths in me will live, even though they die; and whoever lives by faithing in me will never die. Do you faith this?" (11:25–26 PARAPHRASED)

"Yes, Lord," she replied literally, "I faith that you are the Messiah, the Son of God, who is to come into the world."

Martha's confession is one of the great confessions of faith to be found anywhere in the Bible, much less in John. "I faith you are the Christ." After she says this, she goes back and calls her sister Mary aside.

> "The Teacher is here," she said, "and is asking for you." When Mary heard this, she got up quickly and went to him. Now Jesus had not yet entered the village, but was still at the place where Martha had met him. When the Jews who had been with Mary in the house, comforting her, noticed how quickly she got up and went out, they followed her, supposing she was going to the tomb to mourn there.
>
> When Mary reached the place where Jesus was and saw him, she fell at his feet and said, "Lord, if you had been here, my brother would not have died."
>
> When Jesus saw her weeping, and the Jews who had come along with her also weeping, he was deeply moved in spirit and troubled. "Where have you laid him?" he asked.
>
> "Come and see, Lord," they replied.
>
> Jesus wept. (11:28b–35)

As little as John writes about Jesus's humanity, there are few moments where we see genuine human emotions like this.

> Then the Jews said, "See how he loved him!"
>
> But some of them said, "Could not he who opened the eyes of the blind man have kept this man from dying?"
>
> Jesus, once more deeply moved, came to the tomb. It was a cave with a stone laid across the entrance. "Take away the stone," he said.

> "But, Lord," said Martha, the sister of the dead man, "by this time there is a bad odor, for he has been there four days."
>
> Then Jesus said, "Did I not tell you that if you believe, you will see the glory of God?"
>
> So they took away the stone. Then Jesus looked up and said, "Father, I thank you that you have heard me. I knew that you always hear me, but I said this for the benefit of the people standing here, that they may believe that you sent me."
>
> When he had said this, Jesus called in a loud voice, "Lazarus, come out!" The dead man came out, his hands and feet wrapped with strips of linen, and a cloth around his face.
>
> Jesus said to them, "Take off the grave clothes and let him go." (11:36–44)

Does Jesus call out in a loud voice because the dead are notoriously hard of hearing? And does he call Lazarus by name so others in tombs won't come out and treat us to a zombie movie rather than a single awesome raising of a dead man?

It's a great story, but that's not the end of it. We have this wonderful little addition to the story in John 12. After Jesus has raised Lazarus from the dead, they have a party, and if they were British, they'd be singing to Jesus and Lazarus, "For he's a jolly good fellow." Both men seem to be guests of honor at this little shindig, a celebration of the raiser and the raised.

People come to the party, not just to see Jesus, but to see Lazarus whom he had raised from the dead. If you arrived at this party to find two receiving lines—one for Lazarus and one for Jesus—which line would you join? Whom would you want to talk to first?

You can join the line to talk to Jesus first. We'll be there in a minute.

We're in the line to speak to Lazarus first.

We have some questions. How often do we get to talk to an expert in death? All those questions you ever wanted to know the answer to, Lazarus has the answers.

Was there a bright light?

Does Wednesday night Bible study attendance count?

All the things you want to know, Lazarus can tell you. A large crowd of Jews find out that Jesus is there and come out not only because of him but also to see Lazarus. The next thing that happens is not funny. It's wickedly funny. The chief priests start planning to return Lazarus to the tomb where he came from. They plot to kill Jesus *and* Lazarus. For, on account of Lazarus, many of the Jews are going over to Jesus and faithing him.

Do you see anything wrong with this strategy of the Jewish religious leaders? Jesus has just raised Lazarus from the dead, and they're thinking about returning Lazarus to the tomb?

Kill Lazarus. Raise Lazarus. Kill Lazarus. Raise him. It's not only silly but it shows in John that unbelief, unfaithing, often has a nasty moral component as well. Opponents of Jesus see plainly that Lazarus has been raised, but they are still blind to the sign that proves Jesus truly is the Messiah. So they plot to kill Lazarus to destroy the evidence. How much evidence is needed to convince these folks that Jesus is the Messiah? Never enough. No amount of evidence would ever do, because they are already trying to destroy the ample evidence they have.

The story is not about Lazarus or about opponents who deny Jesus and try to kill the evidence that he's the Messiah. This story is primarily about Martha, and it is written for people like us who need daring faith like hers.

When Jesus gets to the tomb, what he does rings a clear bell of memory of the conversation Martha and Jesus had on the road, of Martha's confession, and Jesus's promise, "Your brother will rise again." It wasn't just a symbolic or theoretical conversation. Do you faith this?

This story is about a moment for each of us: will we faith Jesus or not? The story is not about whether Martha believes in the Messiah. It's obvious she does. The question of the story is, Will she faith it or not?

If we went around the room and asked everybody to say what you believe about Jesus, we would say remarkably similar things. I believe in Jesus. Yes, me too. For John, the question is not simply "Do you believe?" but the larger question is this: When crucial moments in your life occur, will you faith Jesus? When you lose that job you never thought you would lose. When you have the disease you never thought you would have. When your child dies. Or on the other end of the spectrum, when you win the lottery with a ticket you found on the church parking lot—because you *never* would have bought *a lottery ticket*—will you faith Jesus or not? Sometimes faithing in the good moments is harder than faithing in the tough times.

For John, this story is not primarily about those obstinate unbelievers. Evidence doesn't ever seem to convince them that

Jesus is the Messiah. The question is this: Are those of us who say we are believers in Jesus willing to faith it in the tough moments *and* in the good moments when we often forget Jesus?

There's that moment at the tomb when Jesus says, "Didn't I tell you that if you faithed me, you would see the glory of God?" It wasn't a theological conversation; it wasn't a theoretical conversation; it was about a way of life. The question was about faithing your way through life.

One more time, remember our opening proposal that the reason John wrote this book is because Christians were getting kicked out of the synagogues, toppled out of their social, religious, and economic lives. It's as if he's just looking at them and saying, Now that it's getting tough, are you going to faith it or not? That's what Jesus's greatest miracle is really about. It's not so much about Lazarus; it's about Martha, and it's about whether or not we will faith the truth she preaches.

TRUTH & DARE

DARE SEVEN

Read John 11:1–12:11

1. What do you dislike and like about the story?

2. What specific action or inaction does God seem to want from you, from others, from the church?

3. What actions, words, attitudes of yours are not obedient to this teaching you've read today?

4. Who is a person with whom God wants you to share what you've learned from the Gospel of John this week?

DARE EIGHT:
Lord and Servant

"The world tells us to seek success, power, and money; God tells us to seek humility, service, and love."
—Pope Francis

ONE OF THE STORIES JOHN TELLS LEADING UP TO the crucifixion of Jesus is about Jesus washing his apostles' feet. The story is far more than just a nice, warm story; it tells us something fundamental about the identity of Jesus. In the story of Jesus feeding the multitudes, we saw how the crowd wants to make him king, and Jesus refuses and slips away. Instead of being crowned king, Jesus says, "I am the bread of life." In some ways, John 13 is an extension of that act of reversal. The apostles have just argued about who is the greatest among them, and Jesus, the Word, gives up on words and decides to show them how to be the greatest.

When we hear that the apostles have been arguing about who is the greatest, we often think it's such a junior high argument. Seriously? They're *with* the LORD, and they are arguing about who's next in line! On second thought, if you were an apostle Jesus hung out with, you . . . don't . . . think . . . you too would . . . wonder . . . who Jesus likes most?

Truly, don't we engage in the same kind of arguments, just in different ways? In a mother's-day-out, who has the best-behaved child? Who's the best disciplinarian? Who is so smart in all the little teaching moments spoken to the toddler loud enough for everyone in the grocery store to hear and be impressed with your parental wisdom?

Don't we try to be the greatest at work? Make the biggest contribution at church so the preacher or elders can see us and give us points? Points for *what*, we don't know, but we still want those points. We want to be caught serving, if we serve much at all. Serving feels so good, but it would feel so much better if some key people saw me serving. Is my idea valued most? Will my idea be the one that the boss stands up in the meeting and applauds? Bravo! When will I become equal partner? It's not about the money, it's just, you know, I need some R-E-S-P-E-C-T.

How many times do people in roles as varied as ministers to doctors to contractors part ways because they cannot get along, can't work out their differences? Their differences, we guess, did not have to do with *giving too much grace* to one another. Grandparents, you *do not* want to be the second-fiddle grandparents. Moms and dads compete, both divorced and married parents, for who is MVP (Most Valuable Parent). We may give gifts or serve out of the goodness of our hearts or to help someone, but in our hearts, do we also fear that we may not always be the greatest in the hearts of those we love?

So, maybe we ought to lay off criticizing the apostles. Let's talk about us. Talking about us is not trying to play into the narcissism of the age, but we're pushing back against the judgmental arrogance of liberals, conservatives . . . and you moderates, too—we can all be arrogant. Humans fairly naturally believe our position is the greatest, and we need this reality check Jesus serves up and John 13 describes.

So, take off your shoes. This is holy ground, and God is about to wash all of our nasty feet. Jesus shows his apostles, and us, an alternative to all the elbowing we just described in our lives.

> It was just before the Passover Festival. Jesus knew that the hour had come for him to leave this world and go to the Father. Having loved his own who were in the world, he loved them to the end.
>
> The evening meal was in progress, and the devil had already prompted Judas, the son of Simon Iscariot, to betray Jesus. Jesus knew that the Father had put all things under his power, and that he had come from God and was returning to God; so he got up from the meal, took off his outer clothing, and wrapped a towel around his waist. After that, he poured water into a basin and began to wash his disciples' feet, drying them with the towel that was wrapped around him. (13:1–5)

John leads into this story by saying that Jesus has all power and authority. Not only does he reject being the kind of king people expect, but he also empties himself of the power described here and becomes a servant to his apostles. If we were writing John's introduction to the story, we would make a big point to transition between these two big ideas: first, the Father had put all things under his power, and second, he washed dirty feet. If we were writing it, we'd have put a huge disclaimer to lead the sentence: *In spite of the fact that* the Father had put all things under his power, he *still* washed the disciples' dirty feet.

John doesn't write it that way. Depending on how it's translated, there's either no transition or a simple, "so," as if it's the most logical thing in the world to have all power in the universe and *therefore*, naturally, the next thing he does is to wash people's feet.

What if you were given infinite power and authority today? What's your first move with your newfound power? Given such power, we know what we'd do nine times out of eight. Buy a deserted island, build a tree house with indoor plumbing and a hammock. We wouldn't really need to rule the world, just an island, and we think we deserve WiFi on the island as well.

Maybe this tendency to misuse perceived power is the reason some churches have annual ceremonial foot washing. Some churches do this on the Thursday before Easter, also called Maundy Thursday. Still, we have no way to duplicate today what was happening in the story of Jesus washing the apostles' feet.

We eat at tables and sit on chairs, so our feet are tucked under the table, and nobody particularly cares if your feet are clean or not. In the ancient world, they ate at low tables as they reclined and folded their legs back or to the side. Your feet could be really close to someone's face. It's not like today where we have our shoes and socks on, and we're walking on sidewalks and tile. No, you are walking on dirt roads, in sandals, so when you go to somebody's house to eat, the host will have one of the household servants wash your dirty feet so you'll be more pleasant to be with at the table. This is an awkward situation, because here they are in this upstairs room. It's a meeting house with no one living there to play host. So there's no household servant, nobody to do the absolutely necessary task of washing feet before they eat.

Can you imagine this awkward social situation? You have Jesus and the apostles standing around and everybody's wondering, "Who's gonna wash our feet?" If you take on the initiative to become the foot-washer, you're basically saying, with reference to everyone else in the room, "I'm taking the slave's spot. I'm taking the servant's place. I'm taking the lowest spot. I'm losing that argument we just had, for sure. It would not resemble that American, pseudo-humble, CEO-gettin'-dirty, hardhat-for-the-day mentality. *Let me get that basin. Take off your shoes. Are the cameras rolling?* No, washing feet in Jesus's day would serve to prove you really aren't leadership material in the expected revolution.

We imagine a tax collector thinking, *I hope the Zealot does it.* The Zealot is thinking, *It's obvious the tax collector is the lowest on the social ladder here. Does anyone doubt that? So, why doesn't he make the move!?*

As they stand around wondering who is going to wash their feet, it goes from awkward to humiliating when Jesus says, "I'm going to wash your feet."

Now the apostles could be thinking, *It was bad a moment ago, but now it's even worse, because our Rabbi is disrobing.*

Though this is a symbolic act, it is still a real act of service. Jesus is doing what is needed in the situation, and it is not a task anybody particularly wants to do.

So Jesus has this bowl of water and a towel wrapped around him, probably one of those hotel towels that's big enough to wipe your face while it's wrapped around you, and he pours water into the bowl and begins washing the disciples' feet and drying them with the big towel.

> He came to Simon Peter, who said to him, "Lord, are you going to wash my feet?"
>
> Jesus replied, "You do not realize now what I am doing, but later you will understand."
>
> "No," said Peter, "you shall never wash my feet."
>
> Jesus answered, "Unless I wash you, you have no part with me."
>
> "Then, Lord," Simon Peter replied, "not just my feet but my hands and my head as well!" (11:6–9)

Peter's response is a classic turnabout, here loosely translated: "Don't even think about getting me wet! What's that? No part of you if you don't wash my feet? Oh, well in that case, drench me!"

> Jesus answered, "Those who have had a bath need only
> to wash their feet; their whole body is clean. And you are
> clean, though not every one of you." For he knew who
> was going to betray him, and that was why he said not
> everyone was clean.
>
> When he had finished washing their feet, he put on
> his clothes and returned to his place. "Do you under-
> stand what I have done for you?" he asked them. "You
> call me 'Teacher' and 'Lord,' and rightly so, for that is
> what I am." (13:10–13)

For Jesus, his service flows out of this identity as Teacher and
Lord.

> "Now that I, your Lord and Teacher, have washed your
> feet, you also should wash one another's feet. I have set
> you an example that you should do as I have done for
> you. Very truly I tell you, no servant is greater than his
> master, nor is a messenger greater than the one who sent
> him. Now that you know these things, you will be blessed
> if you do them." (13:14–17)

What Jesus does is particularly important for those who have
positions and titles of leadership to notice. For Jesus, the titles
Teacher and Lord do not exclude or rule out identity as Servant.
The act of washing feet is told in John as if such humbling
service is a natural extension of Jesus knowing who he is and
where he's going. Foot-washing is an extension of Jesus's identity as the One sent from God. So from a human perspective
we're asking why a king would act like a houseboy, but thinking

"from above" reminds us that if we do not get the incredible irony of Jesus as a slave, then we are still cold to the trail of following the true Jesus.

In our ministries both of us occasionally serve people. Both of us admit that there are times when we don't serve inside out. We see something that needs to be done, and we think, *Okay, they need this done and I can do it, so I'll do it. There it's done.*

John seems to suggest that if you want to be a follower of Jesus, then you have to serve people inside out. What we mean by "serving inside out" is that the serving flows from your true identity. You are empowered to serve when you know who you are and where you are going. Just to make sure that we don't miss the point, Jesus ties his action with a proclamation about who he is, what he's done, what they ought to do in response, and what will happen if they do.

Most of us can think of at least one person for whom service to other people is a natural extension of their identity. It's not as if they have to think about it; it's not as if they worry about their status or their place. They know who they are, so they serve out of this identity.

Both of us live in a scholarly world, so we know there is nothing more aggravating than scholars who are insecure about their scholarship, because they have to constantly try to prove themselves to you. When you are working with people who know who they are and know where they're going, they don't have to prove anything to you. Jesus has such a deep sense of his identity with God that caring for people around him is the natural extension of his identity.

Occasionally in our churches and small groups we agree on a little rule before we start a potluck meal. You can't serve yourself. You have to get someone else's food for them. You have to think about the people around you and what they need. So we give the persistent dominance of our own needs a rest and allow someone else to care for us.

What would happen if we became the kind of people who were so secure in our own identity that when we walked into a room, our eyes constantly would watch as we think, *What do people need? How can I serve them?* We know people who have their head on a swivel, constantly looking for the outcast, the loner, the needy. Do you know someone like this in your church, workplace, family, or neighborhood?

Jesus shows us how to do this. He does not act like a Teacher and Lord who demands that everybody serve him and treat him with deference. He's the one washing feet.

Are you a staff minister at a church? Have you exchanged this way of Jesus for the belief that you must constantly have people treat you with deference and respect, always serving your needs so you can "do ministry"? We mention this because we've been tempted to act this way. No doubt, we have acted this way at times. When you get tenure at a university or finally work your way in a church from youth minister to associate minister to pulpit minister, you've done your time. Servant? *I'd rather be Teacher and Lord so I can flaunt my tenure, education, and depths of wisdom over the flock!* Are you above serving in the food pantry to serve the poor, because that has been duly delegated to others?

Are you an owner of a business? Do you know the people who produce the product you sell and the conditions in which they work? Are you a dad who comes home and expects to be served rather than to help with the dishes, simply because, "hey, I work for a living"? Are you a teenager who thinks because you have schoolwork and club soccer that you have no time to serve? Lots of people want to serve meals on Thanksgiving Day to homeless people, and that is kind, but what are we doing the other three hundred sixty-four days of the year?

Pray a simple prayer that reminds us that the fullness of God washed human feet.

"Father, in the name of Jesus the Servant Son through the power of the Holy Spirit, make me a servant like you. Show me daring new ways to get over my hang-ups and pompous nature, fear, worry about position, and serve people like you did in Christ on earth."

There's something else that happens in the story after Jesus washes feet. After he does this humble act of service, he is betrayed by one of his disciples. Jesus knows his betrayer, even gives him a blessing of sorts when he dips bread in a sauce and hands it to Judas Iscariot. At that point, Judas had already sold Jesus out for thirty pieces of silver to the Jewish ruling council that was plotting to turn Jesus over to the Roman authorities to have him crucified. John shows Jesus in complete control. Jesus isn't sold out without his knowledge and willingness to go along with it.

The act of foot-washing leads to the cross. The One who has chosen to wash feet, also chooses to lay his life down for the sin of the world. No one takes his life from him.

John omits the greatest command that we find in other Gospels. He opts for showing us in this story of washing feet what true love looks like. John re-words the greatest two commands, love God and love your neighbor, into what he calls "a new command."

"A new command I give you: Love one another. As I have loved you, so you must love one another. By this everyone will know that you are my disciples, if you love one another" (13:34–35). Peter seems to miss this final command of Jesus and says he will lay down his life for Jesus! Jesus is incredulous. "Will you really lay down your life for me, Peter? Truly, before dawn, before you hear the rooster crow three times, you will deny me three times."

Our service flows out of who we are, and Jesus says if we obey this command to serve one another, the world sees a community of love and knows we are Christ's disciples. This serving love is another way to bear witness to the world that Christ is truly the Son of God. Then Jesus reminds us, "You will be blessed if you do them."

Identity of a Servant

I frequently visit Allelon House, a place of intentional community. *Allelon* is the Greek word for "One Another." There are different guys who have lived there over the years, but they've always been committed to the same thing. How do they serve one another? How do they serve the people of their community?

Hundreds, maybe thousands, of people have come to this house to share a meal and fellowship. More people may come through this house in a month than we typically have in our own houses in a year. In a real way, this house and the people who live in community here are an embodiment of the story of Jesus washing feet (John 13). The Allelon community shows us what it means to let this text become real in our lives. There's a good reason why this has been one of the most compelling texts in the Bible, why people have returned to it again and again.

The story has everything to do with hospitality. The apostles of Jesus have gathered together in a room, and there's no obvious host. Or better put, there are no obvious servants. So the question arises, "Who's going to take the place of the servant? Who's going to offer hospitality?" Who's going to be on the receiving end? Who's going to be on the giving end? One of the most compelling stories in the whole Bible is this one that helps us visualize Jesus Christ, Lord and Master, as servant of all.

I've been in the Allelon house when it's noisy and filled with children, and I've been in the house when it's quiet. In either case, there is a lot of peace here, even when kids are running everywhere and people have come to share a meal. They come to share stories. You can see Allelon House—in quiet and noisy times—in our previous video series, *Living Jesus.*

In the quiet, after we look at this text, we probably need to sit all by ourselves and think about who we are and where we get our identity. Do we get our identity from how much of the world we control, or do we get our identity from how much of the world we serve?

—*Randy*

DARE EIGHT

TRUTH & DARE

Read John 13:1–38

1. What do you dislike and like about the story of Jesus washing feet?

2. What specific action or inaction does God seem to want from you, from others, from the church?

3. What actions, words, attitudes of yours are not obedient to this teaching you've read today?

4. Who is a person with whom God wants you to share what you've learned from the Gospel of John this week?

5. If you'd been given all power and authority like Jesus, what would you do with this power?

6. Pray this simple prayer: "Father, in the name of Jesus the Servant Son through the power of the Holy Spirit, make me a servant like you."

7. Who is someone who has personified Jesus by "washing your feet"—literally or figuratively in service to you?

DARE NINE:
The Holy Spirit

> "[Gospel teaching] insists that no one can take credit for belief. One cannot boast, 'I have decided to have faith,' for faith is always at least in large part a gift from God. On the other hand, the Gospel persists in holding humans responsible for unbelief. We cannot boast of our faith, but neither can we excuse our lack of faith. We are left to ponder the paradox."
> —Robert Kysar

ANOTHER STRANGE THING ABOUT JOHN IS THAT he's the only Gospel writer who talks much about the Holy Spirit. In fact, other than Paul (and Luke in Acts), John is the only writer in the Bible who talks extensively about the Holy Spirit. What is John's goal in writing about the Holy Spirit?

John uses a strange word in Greek to refer to the Holy Spirit: *paraclete*. In English this term is translated one of two ways: "advocate" or "counselor." John could have both meanings in mind when he uses the word in John 14–16.

If you ever get into serious trouble, one variable in your courtroom experience will impact your prison time or freedom most: your legal counsel. Think about the notion of the

Holy Spirit being your defense attorney. We're feeling better about life already. How about you?

You can also think about the *paraclete* as a counselor. Why do you go to a counselor? Some persist in thinking of a counselor as someone you need only when you are in crisis, but a counselor is someone who helps you think rationally, who helps you get in touch with feelings you have allowed to impact you negatively, and who helps you discern wisely what's going on in your life. The *paraclete* could fit nicely into one or all of these categories of assistance. In the case of the Counselor whom Jesus is talking about, it's not some sort of rent-a-friend counsel but someone who can actually help out.

So you have the Holy Spirit who will be by your side like an attorney or a counselor who has your back. In fact, the word *paraclete* has the idiomatic sense of "someone who comes alongside you." The Holy Spirit is going to be your advocate in court; he's going to be the one who will give you wise counsel. That's the way John thinks about the Holy Spirit. So, as you read 14:15–27 below, think of the Holy Spirit as your attorney, your counselor who comes beside.

> "If you love me, keep my commands. And I will ask the Father, and he will give you another advocate to help you and be with you forever—the Spirit of truth. The world cannot accept him, because it neither sees him nor knows him. But you know him, for he lives with you and will be in you. I will not leave you as orphans; I will come to you. Before long, the world will not see me anymore, but you will see me. Because I live, you also will live. On

that day you will realize that I am in my Father, and you are in me, and I am in you. Whoever has my commands and keeps them is the one who loves me. The one who loves me will be loved by my Father, and I too will love them and show myself to them."

Then Judas (not Judas Iscariot) said, "But, Lord, why do you intend to show yourself to us and not to the world?"

Jesus replied, "Anyone who loves me will obey my teaching. My Father will love them, and we will come to them and make our home with them. Anyone who does not love me will not obey my teaching. These words you hear are not my own; they belong to the Father who sent me.

"All this I have spoken while still with you. But the Advocate, the Holy Spirit, whom the Father will send in my name, will teach you all things and will remind you of everything I have said to you. Peace I leave with you; my peace I give you. I do not give to you as the world gives. Do not let your hearts be troubled and do not be afraid."

One of the big reasons Jesus is telling the apostles about the Helper is so they will not fall away under persecution. He says they will be put out of the synagogue and people who kill them will think they are doing God a great service. Then he says in 16:6–15,

Rather, you are filled with grief because I have said these things. But very truly I tell you, it is for your good that I am going away. Unless I go away, the Advocate will not come to you; but if I go, I will send him to you. When he comes, he will prove the world to be in the wrong about sin and righteousness and judgment: about sin, because people do not believe in me; about righteousness, because I am going to the Father, where you can see me no longer; and about judgment, because the prince of this world now stands condemned.

"I have much more to say to you, more than you can now bear. But when he, the Spirit of truth, comes, he will guide you into all the truth. He will not speak on his own; he will speak only what he hears, and he will tell you what is yet to come. He will glorify me because it is from me that he will receive what he will make known to you. All that belongs to the Father is mine. That is why I said the Spirit will receive from me what he will make known to you."

These are complicated teachings on the Holy Spirit, but the most helpful thing we can say is that they are spoken to disciples who are about to enter great persecution. Did you notice that the disciples keep asking Jesus where he's going? Children often do that with parents when they leave the room or the house. "Dad, where are you going?" Children often experience what psychologists call "separation anxiety." They need the security of the parent with them, and Jesus assures them that he will not leave them as orphans, that another Counselor is coming to be with them. One of the great recurring themes of Scripture is that there is always some presence of God in the world with his people.

The Holy Spirit, however, is sent not simply to protect, comfort, and come alongside us. A leading role of the Holy Spirit is to bear witness to Jesus and what he taught. Some Christians get so enamored with the notion of the Holy Spirit that he becomes the center of their theology. Jesus makes it clear, however, that the Holy Spirit is not the true center of theology. The Holy Spirit does not point to himself. The Holy Spirit always points to Jesus. Jesus says the Holy Spirit "will guide you into all the truth." That's the work of the Spirit.

John is trying to inspire daring faith in a Savior his readers and hearers (including us) never saw. Remember this Gospel was written in about 85 AD, so it's a second generation document written to people who never laid eyes on Jesus. We want this idea to bring us a step closer to these early Christians who read John the way we do, blessed to be those who do not see and yet believe!

The fact that you are reading a book like ours and have come this far means you are deeply interested in Jesus, believe in Jesus, and want daring faith. How do we get from thinking all this is "probably true" to a life of deep commitment, to a life of faithing? John has the answer. The way you get to that life of deep commitment is the Holy Spirit in you, who bears witness that these things are true.

Do you believe in the living Lord because of the resurrection? Or do you believe in the resurrection because of the living Lord? The only right answer to that two-part question is, Yes. You believe on the testimony of history, but you also believe because the Holy Spirit within you bears witness to the truth.

For John, this is a way to bridge the gap of unbelief. We already have a perceived delay of Jesus's return, even as early as in John's time. Many early Christians thought Jesus was coming back quickly. It seems they thought the Christian journey is a sprint, not a marathon. When John pens his Gospel, years have passed, decades, and now half a century since Jesus ascended. Can we really believe this? John says yes, because he has given you this Spirit that continues to bear witness to you that these things are true.

The Holy Spirit is a gift to believers. The Holy Spirit's relationship with the world is to convict the world of sin. A world that doesn't recognize Jesus is not going to recognize the Holy Spirit, either. The Holy Spirit is actually One who needs our cooperation.

Just as a lawyer needs your cooperation as his client, just as your counselor is not going to work harder than you, so the Spirit works most powerfully through Christians' daring faith.

Would you rather have Jesus alongside you or the Holy Spirit? Many of us can visualize Jesus better because of the Gospel stories. Jesus has the nerve to say, however, that "it's better for you that I go." When it comes to the Holy Spirit, I can be with you always, wherever you are, all the time. God decided the physical Jesus would be one man in one place. And God also decided to send another Comforter, Advocate, Counselor, who is going to be with us to the end. He is the continuing presence of Jesus in our lives.

How do we have this kind of relationship with Father, Son, and Holy Spirit? William Barclay, in his book *The Gospel of John,* said, "The secret of the life of Jesus was his contact with

God; again and again he withdrew into a solitary place to meet him. We must keep contact with Jesus. We cannot do that unless we deliberately take some steps to do it." Arrange your life, Barclay continues, so that "there's never a day when we give ourselves a chance to forget him" (205).

Jesus calls this way of arranging your life, this constant connection with him, "remaining" or "abiding," depending on the version of the Bible you read. In 15:1–11 Jesus says "remain" eleven times.

> I am the true vine, and my Father is the gardener. He cuts off every branch in me that bears no fruit, while every branch that does bear fruit he prunes so that it will be even more fruitful. You are already clean because of the word I have spoken to you. Remain in me, as I also remain in you. No branch can bear fruit by itself; it must remain in the vine. Neither can you bear fruit unless you remain in me.
>
> I am the vine; you are the branches. If you remain in me and I in you, you will bear much fruit; apart from me you can do nothing. If you do not remain in me, you are like a branch that is thrown away and withers; such branches are picked up, thrown into the fire and burned. If you remain in me and my words remain in you, ask whatever you wish, and it will be done for you. This is to my Father's glory, that you bear much fruit, showing yourselves to be my disciples.
>
> As the Father has loved me, so have I loved you. Now remain in my love. If you keep my commands, you will

> remain in my love, just as I have kept my Father's com-
> mands and remain in his love. I have told you this so that
> my joy may be in you and that your joy may be complete.

Teresa of Avila has a centuries-old book in which she develops the concept of remaining or abiding with Jesus in mansion rooms that represent a deepening relationship with Father, Son, and Holy Spirit. The idea of rooms comes from Jesus in 14:2: "Do not let your hearts be troubled. You believe in God; believe also in me. My Father's house has many rooms; if that were not so, would I have told you that I am going there to prepare a place for you?"

Tom Ashbrook, in his helpful book, *Mansions of the Heart,* brings a contemporary application to Teresa's mansions, show-ing how each room represents a deepening relationship step with Father, Son, and Holy Spirit. He says, "God's ultimate goal for your life is for you to live fully and freely in his love, and to respond by loving him as well. He has no ulterior motives; he just wants you to be his son, daughter, friend, co-worker in love."

Jesus is showing us discipleship that flows out of an abid-ing relationship with God. If the ideas and works of Teresa of Avila or Tom Ashbrook sound heavy or mystical, you may want to read a brief sketch of the metaphor of the Vine in John 15 by Bruce Wilkerson, *Secrets of the Vine.* One of the things we've learned from this book is that abiding is not about doing more *for* God but being more *with* him, and this abiding—and occasional pruning and chastening when we disobey—leads to greater fruitfulness.

It's interesting that what Jesus offers as comfort, the Holy Spirit, has in our world become more of an object of controversy.

What does the Holy Spirit do, how does the Holy Spirit express himself, are we going to be charismatic or non-charismatic? People may find theoretical answers to these questions but miss remaining or abiding with the living Spirit of God who Christ has endorsed as the Counselor who walks beside us. We can let go of some of these questions or issues, but Jesus's promise that there will be a continuing presence of God in our lives is worth holding on to.

The Way (John 14:4–6)

We give Thomas a bad rap, call him doubter. I'd rather call him Honest Thomas. When Jesus says the disciples know the way, Thomas is transparent. "Jesus, uh, we do not know the way, so . . ."

What Jesus comes back with is one of Christianity's all-time high-water-mark Scriptures, next to John 3:16 in popularity and familiarity. Jesus says to Thomas: "I am the way, the truth, and the life. No one comes to the Father except through me."

William Barclay says this is a great saying to us but would be greater still for Jews hearing it for the first time. Why is that? Barclay says Jesus took three of the great basic conceptions of Judaism and made the tremendous claim that in himself all three—way, truth, life—find their full realization. From Moses to psalmists to Isaiah, the Jews spoke frequently about the way of God (Deut. 5:32–33; Ps. 27:11; Isa. 30:21).

Isaiah said that in this new way travelers would not become lost (Isa. 35:8).

Everyone has had the experience of trying to follow someone's directions. But the best way to not get lost is when someone giving directions simply says, "Come on, I'll just take you there." Barclay says, "That is what Jesus does for us. He does not only give advice and directions. He takes us by the hand and leads us; he strengthens us and guides us personally every day. He does not tell us about the way; he is the Way."

In a similar way, Jesus is not simply a great teacher who teaches us doctrines to believe. Barclay continues, "No teacher has ever embodied the truth he taught—except Jesus. Many a man could say: 'I have taught you the truth.' Only Jesus could say: 'I am the Truth.' The tremendous thing about Jesus is not simply that the statement of moral perfection finds its peak in him; it is that the fact of moral perfection finds its realization in him."

Finally, God in Christ does more than create life, but shows us the whole of life from birth, life, death, resurrection, and eternal reign. All of life has been laid out before us in Christ. What the psalmist saw: "Thou dost show me the path of life" (Psalm 16:11), Jesus became for us: "I am the Life." Jesus came to bring that kind of life, so strong that he could say, "There's no other way to the Father except through me."

Eugene H. Peterson makes a strong connection between what philosopher Heraclitus once said and this text in John 14:6. "The way up and the way down is the same way." Peterson observes that the way we come to the Father is the same way the Father comes to us: in Jesus. Jesus does not merely point the way and give us a map. He goes with us, yet he is also the destination. Jesus *is* the way. Jesus does not merely teach truth. He embodies truth. Jesus *is* the truth. Jesus does not just give life or give us advice about how to live good lives. He is what true life looks like. Jesus himself *is* life.

Jesus does not merely point to the way, teach truth, and give life-lessons. Jesus has come into the world to become the way to the Father.

Christians often agonize over Jesus saying, "No one comes to the Father, except through me."

We dare you to release yourself from carrying the weight of the words of Jesus and instead let Jesus speak them into *your own* life. Come to the Father through Jesus and find the truth in what Jesus is saying. Then and only then will you have the wisdom to know how to apply this to evangelism, talking to a Hindu or a Muslim. No one will believe these words because you make it a bumper sticker or a Facebook post. People will believe it when Christians walk the way of Jesus who said,

> The reason my Father loves me is that I lay down my life—only to take it up again. No one takes it from me, but I lay it down of my own accord. I have authority to lay it down and authority to take it up again. This command I received from my Father. (10:17–18)

After Jesus said all these words, he was tortured and killed rather than doing violence against his own creation, thereby showing the greatest extent of God's love. The truth that he overcame the power of death is embodied in an empty tomb. And the life that he still lives proves he continues to be the way to the Father, reigning at the right hand of the Father even now and forever as the King of the Universe.

—Greg

TRUTH & DARE

DARE NINE

Read John 14–16.

1. What words or phrases do you notice as you read John 14–16?
2. What do you dislike and like about the story?
3. What does God seem to be showing about himself, ourselves, the world?
4. Pray for wisdom as you read John 14–16. The same counselor will guide you in all truth.
5. What specific action or inaction does God seem to want from you, from others, from the church?
6. What actions, words, attitudes of yours are not obedient to this teaching you've read today?
7. Who is a person with whom God wants you to share what you've learned from the Gospel of John this week?

DARE TEN:
Living the Prayer of Jesus

"There is no voice which has ever been heard,
either in heaven or in earth, more exalted, more holy,
more fruitful, more sublime, than the prayer offered
up by the Son to God Himself."
—Philip Melanchthon

IF YOU'RE GOING TO DO AN EXPLOSION, YOU WANT to have a physicist nearby. You want him to understand what compounds you're using and how they are going to react. And if you have someone who knows what they are doing, explosions can actually be reasonably predictable. But that's not quite true when you put the combustible element of different kinds of Christians together.

Even in Jesus's day there was already a problem with those who identified other followers of Jesus as the enemy rather than their friends. And sometimes when you put people like that together, what you get are very unpredictable explosions.

What we get is not something created in unity. What we get is something terribly destructive.

Jesus prays differently in John from how he prays in Matthew, Mark, and Luke. In John, for example, we don't have those agonizing moments of prayer in the garden where Jesus is wrestling with God. Is there a reason we don't see an anguished Jesus praying, "Father, if you are willing, take this cup from me; yet not my will, but yours be done"? Remember, John shows Jesus in control of everything. The prayers in the synoptics seem to show weakness. John does not have these prayers, but John does have one long prayer of Jesus, the one found in John 17. It is framed as prayer, with Jesus speaking to the Father, but it doesn't sound very much like a prayer. What it sounds like is a sermon disguised as a prayer.

Parents, have you ever prayed this kind of disguised prayer? You sit down at the dinner table with your three children, and they are arguing and complaining. How do you pray?

"Lord, our family needs your help to treat one another with love and respect!" Our words communicate a sermon to the children as well as a prayer.

Many of us will remember *that old guy* in church worship services whose prayers we timed, to see if he could set a new prayer-length record. He exhorted and corrected most of the congregation and the world at large. The worship order read "Prayer," but what we got was a sermonella disguised as prayer. Whether it's a parent or that old guy, the desire seems to be to bring people together.

The prayer of Jesus is like that. It is addressed to God, so it has the form of a prayer, but it really looks and feels more like a sermon. Whether John 17 is a prayer or sermon, Jesus's desire for his people to be one as he and his Father are one comes through loud and clear. The reason we introduce the prayer this way is to get us ready to hear it both ways: as prayer *and* sermon. Here is what Jesus says.

> After Jesus said this, he looked toward heaven
> and prayed:
> "Father, the hour has come. Glorify your Son, that
> your Son may glorify you. For you granted him authority
> over all people that he might give eternal life to all those
> you have given him. Now this is eternal life: that they
> know you, the only true God, and Jesus Christ, whom
> you have sent. I have brought you glory on earth by
> finishing the work you gave me to do. And now, Father,
> glorify me in your presence with the glory I had with you
> before the world began. (17:1–5)

Did you notice the word "glory"? In John, when Jesus talks about glory, it is always a reference to the cross. Mark's Gospel refers to the cross, but it always associates the cross with shame. In John, the cross is associated with glory. It's as if Jesus is saying, "My greatest moment is when these people think they're killing me. That's precisely when we are going to conquer the world. It's going to be my moment of greatest glory."

> "I have revealed you to those whom you gave me out
> of the world. They were yours; you gave them to me
> and they have obeyed your word. Now they know that
> everything you have given me comes from you. For I

gave them the words you gave me and they accepted
them. They knew with certainty that I came from you,
and they believed that you sent me. I pray for them. I am
not praying for the world, but for those you have given
me, for they are yours. All I have is yours, and all you
have is mine. And glory has come to me through them.
I will remain in the world no longer, but they are still in
the world, and I am coming to you. Holy Father, protect
them by the power of your name, the name you gave me,
so that they may be one as we are one. While I was with
them, I protected them and kept them safe by that name
you gave me. None has been lost except the one doomed
to destruction so that Scripture would be fulfilled.

"I am coming to you now, but I say these things while
I am still in the world, so that they may have the full
measure of my joy within them. I have given them your
word and the world has hated them, for they are not of
the world any more than I am of the world. My prayer
is not that you take them out of the world but that you
protect them from the evil one. They are not of the world,
even as I am not of it. Sanctify them by the truth; your
word is truth. As you sent me into the world, I have sent
them into the world. For them I sanctify myself, that they
too may be truly sanctified.

"My prayer is not for them alone. I pray also for those
who will believe in me through their message, that all
of them may be one, Father, just as you are in me and
I am in you. May they also be in us so that the world
may believe that you have sent me. I have given them

the glory that you gave me, that they may be one as we are one—I in them and you in me—so that they may be brought to complete unity. Then the world will know that you sent me and have loved them even as you have loved me.

"Father, I want those you have given me to be with me where I am, and to see my glory, the glory you have given me because you loved me before the creation of the world.

"Righteous Father, though the world does not know you, I know you, and they know that you have sent me. I have made you known to them, and will continue to make you known in order that the love you have for me may be in them and that I myself may be in them."
(17:6–26)

John does not record any response by the disciples. Remember, however, the ones to whom John is writing, and what they are going through at that time. He's writing to Christians who are starting to pay the price for being disciples of Jesus. Things are getting rough for disciples of the Messiah. Could it be that John puts this sermon/prayer of Jesus into the text to uphold Christ's disciples and keep them from caving in to persecution?

How do we respond when things get rough, when persecution comes? It's hard enough when persecution is not even part of our faith-life. Have you ever noticed how easy it is for us to get sideways with someone? You are working on something together at work, at church, for a neighborhood project, or at school, and things may go well for a while. Then you run into problems. A decision doesn't go someone's way, or a leader strong-arms others, a member tries to take over where it's not his place. People start snipping and sniping. A great preacher of the past said, "One of the reasons we don't evangelize is because we're all here in our own little huddle, and the reason we're in our own little huddle is because we're afraid if we get out of the huddle, somebody on *our own team* is going to tackle us."

Something like this has probably started to happen in these communities of Christians John is writing to. People on their own team have started to tackle them, so John shows us two things in this prayer.

The first thing John points out to us is that Jesus speaks of glory and how it can be seen so vividly in the cross. He wants second-generation Christians to know that when you start suffering persecution, when the world is kicking you in the teeth, you need to know the thing that draws believers closer: the glory of Jesus. You don't have to be ashamed of the cross. You don't have to be ashamed of anything about the life of Jesus. In fact, look to the life of Jesus to understand that he was hated before we are hated. Just as in his suffering, he was glorified, so also we will glorify God in our suffering. When the world treats you that way, it makes you look shockingly like Jesus, so the way we need to think about persecution is not in terms of shame. Instead, look at suffering as if it is sharing glory with Jesus. This doesn't get really clear until the story progresses, where Jesus predicts his own death and what it means.

Second, not only does John get Christians to think about glory, but he also gets them to think about unity in this prayer. He says one of the primary ways we bear witness to the world is by seeing Jesus and the Father as one. If you want to make a list of all the failings of Christianity for two thousand years, not bearing witness because of our disunity belongs at the top of the list. Could it be that we have failed to see the unity between Father and Son as the core of what it means to be unified? This prayer points to the amazing unity and deep relationship of Father and Son.

We bear witness to the world in our unity—by being one as Jesus and the Father are one. Unity is extraordinarily difficult, and the primary reason it's difficult is because of *you*. There's a great story attributed to G. K. Chesterton, probably because he wrote a book called *What's Wrong with the World?* Someone wrote to the *Times* of London and asked, "What *is* wrong with the world?" and Chesterton, it was said, famously wrote back the reply,

> *Dear Sir,*
> *I am.*
> *Yours,*
> *G. K. Chesterton*

Unity is so difficult and therefore rare—we can't even prove by one of his writings that G.K. Chesterton really actually said this. No human *truly* believes it. We think people around us are wrong. I'm right. Why can't everybody else get it? That's why unity is so difficult. If you would just see that I am right about everything, all of our unity problems would be over! We are not running for Pope, but if one of us is elected, we are prepared to serve. All of Christianity's problems will be solved. We can say that, of course jokingly, but the problem is that many people actually believe it. People believe that if they were in charge of their church, company, or family, they'd solve all the problems, because they are right.

Jesus here presents us with the only possible solution to this problem—that we become so centered in Jesus Christ that we become one as Jesus and the Father are one. We will not come closer to unity by coming closer to one another. Not directly. We will come closer to the kind of unity Jesus prays for if we come closer to the cross. As people worldwide all take steps from different directions to the cross, we come closer to Jesus and his glory. What happens? We're not only coming closer to the cross, to the glory of God, but we also get closer together. That's where unity is to be found. This is Jesus's solution, what he's praying for. If you'll let me be the center, Jesus tells us, then a kind of oneness is possible that is never possible when we're all trying to have our own way.

Jesus says the symbol of this unity is me. Jesus is saying, I find my glory not in becoming your king but in being your slave. Do you remember when I washed your feet? I find my glory not in a throne but on a cross. The cross is my throne. Jesus says, I'll show you how to do this. I am showing you how to lay down your life, and that's true glory. Then what I ask you to do is to surround the cross. Follow me, and when you do that, we become one in a way that we never could have otherwise.

After two thousand years, the dream is still not a reality. Jesus's prayer that we all might be one is still something that stands in our future, not in our present. But it continues to appeal to our imagination: that moment when all Christians will claim each other as brothers and sisters. When the prayer for the unity of all believers will no longer need to be a sermon, because it's a reality. Then God's dream finally comes true.

DARE TEN

Read John 17

1. What words and phrases do you remember after reading Jesus's prayer the first time?

2. What do you dislike and like about this sermon-like prayer of Jesus?

3. What specific action or inaction does this prayer call for in you, in your church?

4. What actions, words, attitudes of yours are not obedient to the prayer of Jesus?

5. Who is a person with whom God wants you to share what you've learned from Jesus's prayer?

6. Have you ever prayed the prayer of Jesus in John 17?

7. What do you think would happen if you began to pray this way in your church or community?

DARE ELEVEN:
The Cross as Glory

"A king who dies on the Cross must be the king of a rather strange kingdom."
—Dietrich Bonhoeffer

FOR MANY CHRISTIANS, THE DOMINANT IMAGE OF the cross is a piece of jewelry worn on a necklace. We've seen a church with a large-screen TV attached to a beautiful cross. But the cross Christ died on was a rough wooden cross. There was nothing beautiful about it. It was an instrument of cruel torturous execution. Yet, the cross became the Christian symbol, and Jesus has an interesting way of talking about the cross. As we saw in the last chapter, the word he uses is "glory." Of all things, the cross would be the place where Jesus would be glorified. What would it mean to look at the cross and not see a piece of jewelry, or even an execution instrument, but instead to see the glory of God?

How can we see the cross in this different light—as something Jesus chooses to embrace, rather than something that victimizes him? When Christians read the story of the cross, they see the story of their salvation. The cross is the story of salvation, yes, but the cross is also about the identity of Jesus Christ. And the cross doesn't just happen to him. He embraces it as part of what it means to display the glory of God. How does this impact our identity as Christ's followers? If Christ claims glory in the cross, should we as his followers also claim glory in the cross? What does it mean for us to form an identity that is cross-shaped, or cruciform? It means the cross becomes not just a way of salvation but a way of life for those who believe. We do not avoid the cross. We embrace the cross, the way of glory through suffering and self-emptying love. This is a much different kind of life from taking the cross for our salvation and moving on to a triumphant life of comfort on earth.

When reporters witness a truly earth-shattering event and they write the story, they only have one thought: *don't mess this up.* Quality news writing often is spare and mostly gives a blow-by-blow account of a dramatic world event. Readers are on the edge of their seats. The event *is* the story. All we want to do is get out of the way of this amazing event of the cross.

That's what John does with the crucifixion. Need he do more?

How can you exaggerate or embellish the most unbelievable event in human history? You tell it, and get out of the way. That's what John is attempting: to tell with few details the most significant event in history. What John wants to stand out is not the details of the story, but he wants us to see something important about Jesus.

So when John writes about the trial and crucifixion of Jesus, he does it in ways that are quite different from the other Gospels. Is there any echo in the room? By this second-to-last chapter of this study, it seems that by now we could leave off the requisite sentence about John's weirdness. There's one theme, however, that comes through over and over and over again. That theme is this: no one does anything to Jesus that he doesn't want to happen. Jesus is absolutely, one hundred percent in control of the situation. We're going to show you just a few passages from the trial and crucifixion of Jesus to illustrate this.

The collection of events around the crucifixion of Jesus is called the "passion" of Jesus. The first episode that shows Jesus is in control is when he is arrested. Some call this the Frankenstein verse, because you see men with torches and weapons at night going to apprehend an innocent man.

> When he had finished praying, Jesus left with his disciples and crossed the Kidron Valley. On the other side there was a garden, and he and his disciples went into it.
>
> Now Judas, who betrayed him, knew the place, because Jesus had often met there with his disciples. So Judas came to the garden, guiding a detachment of soldiers and some officials from the chief priests and the Pharisees. They were carrying torches, lanterns, and weapons.

> Jesus, knowing all that was going to happen to him,
> went out and asked them, "Who is it you want?"
>
> "Jesus of Nazareth," they replied.
>
> "I am he," Jesus said. (And Judas the traitor was
> standing there with them.) When Jesus said, "I am he,"
> they drew back and fell to the ground. (18:1–6)

Judas and a detachment of soldiers come to arrest Jesus. Jesus asks, "Who are you looking for?" and they say, "Jesus of Nazareth." Jesus replies with two words we've discussed earlier in the book: "I am."

Who are you seeking?

Jesus of Nazareth.

I Am.

And then something happens that we only see in John's account of Jesus's arrest: at the mention of "I Am," the soldiers back up and fall to the ground. Maybe John wants us to recall another story when meeting the "I Am" makes someone hit the dirt. Long ago, a voice said, "I Am," and Moses fell face down. That's all you can do in the presence of God when you realize who he is. Jesus is at one time freely admitting he is the person they came to capture, but he is also God-in-the-flesh, I Am. It's ironic that the soldiers fall down. The Temple moguls never bowed before Jesus, but now their lynch mob does.

The next thing that happens is not in the text, but we imagine Jesus thinking, *Come on, get up, this is embarrassing. I can't arrest myself. Come on, let's go. We've got work to do here.* John wants to make it clear that nobody's taking Jesus against his will. He's in control.

In Jesus's imprisonment and trial he is also in control. Pilate is really bothered by Jesus in John's account. He's troubled by the whole conversation he has with Jesus. Pilate wants to let him go, but he's afraid of the Jewish leaders who can create all sorts of problems for him. Pilate says to Jesus, Don't you get this? I have the power to let you go or to have you killed. Pilate is playing the same game murderers may play with their victims. Beg for your life. I have the power to let you go or kill you.

Jesus doesn't flinch. Remember, he's in control. He turns Pilate's words on their head. Power? Any power you have, Buster, comes from above where I come from. You don't have any power on your own. John wants to make sure that we know that they can't arrest Jesus, can't convict him, can't crucify him without Jesus allowing it.

The actual story of the crucifixion also functions to show us that Jesus is dying for us, but most importantly to John, that Jesus lays down his life willingly.

> Finally Pilate handed him over to them to be crucified.
>
> So the soldiers took charge of Jesus. Carrying his own cross, he went out to the place of the Skull (which in Aramaic is called Golgotha). There they crucified him, and with him two others—one on each side and Jesus in the middle.
>
> Pilate had a notice prepared and fastened to the cross. It read: JESUS OF NAZARETH, THE KING OF THE JEWS. Many of the Jews read this sign, for the place where Jesus was crucified was near the city, and the sign

was written in Aramaic, Latin, and Greek. The chief priests of the Jews protested to Pilate, "Do not write 'The King of the Jews,' but that this man claimed to be king of the Jews."

Pilate answered, "What I have written, I have written."

When the soldiers crucified Jesus, they took his clothes, dividing them into four shares, one for each of them, with the undergarment remaining. This garment was seamless, woven in one piece from top to bottom.

"Let's not tear it," they said to one another. "Let's decide by lot who will get it."

This happened that the scripture might be fulfilled that said,

"They divided my clothes among them and cast lots for my garment."

So this is what the soldiers did.

Near the cross of Jesus stood his mother, his mother's sister, Mary the wife of Clopas, and Mary Magdalene. When Jesus saw his mother there, and the disciple whom he loved standing nearby, he said to her, "Woman, here is your son," and to the disciple, "Here is your mother." From that time on, this disciple took her into his home. (19:16–27)

What is Jesus doing while he's on the cross? He's doing domestic relations. "Mary, son. Son, mother." It doesn't look like a suffering Jesus as much as Jesus in control of his household, and the world.

> Later, knowing that everything had now been finished,
> and so that Scripture would be fulfilled, Jesus said, "I am
> thirsty." A jar of wine vinegar was there, so they soaked a
> sponge in it, put the sponge on a stalk of the hyssop plant,
> and lifted it to Jesus' lips. When he had received the
> drink, Jesus said, "It is finished." With that, he bowed his
> head and gave up his spirit. (19:28–30)

In John's world, Jesus was not *really* killed. He decided to die. It's almost as if he's going down his checklist.

Crucifixion.

Gamble for my clothes, check.

John taking care of mother, done.

Oh, yes, I'm thirsty. I almost forgot. Okay, done.

Done.

It is finished.

Having done all that he chooses to do, Jesus gives up his spirit.

It's an absolutely different way to tell the story. It's one of the glorious things about the Gospels: they all give different angles on the story. From John's point of view, the one thing he wants disciples to understand is this: Jesus died the shameful death of the cross because Jesus the Messiah wanted to die the shameful death of the cross. He decided to. He willingly laid down his life for the world. Nobody kills Jesus. Nobody arrests Jesus. Nobody puts him on trial. Nobody beats Jesus without his express permission. He's not a victim.

Jesus is telling a story with his life. When you look at me, he says, don't see a cross or execution. See a throne. See my glory. In the words of Robert Kysar, "The cross of Jesus is his throne." As Dietrich Bonhoeffer suggests, it is a strange kingdom whose king dies on a cross. But the kind of Kingdom Jesus has initiated has a cross for a throne. The cross is God's supreme act of self-revelation. Christ the Son willingly lays down his life—as he had taught his disciples, "Greater love has no one than this, that he lay down his life for his friends." For John, the cross is the divine presence of God on display for the world to see. This is the fulfillment of what God intended for the divine Word who became flesh.

There is nothing sadder than people using their perceived power over people to do bad things. Yet, nothing is more glorious than when someone has power and lays it down for the sake of those with little or no power. That's the story John wants to tell. Jesus has all the power and authority in the world. Jesus can fell soldiers with the words, "I Am." Jesus can feed multitudes. Jesus can raise a rotting corpse. After *that,* do we really need to give more examples of power? But this story of Lazarus is exactly how John ends his examples of people encountering Jesus, before leading into Jesus's time in Jerusalem, his final teachings and passion. Jesus who can do all this, who has all this power, laid down his life willingly. He *decided* he would die for you.

When John tells the story of the resurrection, we're not surprised because Jesus has been in control of this story all the way. We know how it's going to end because nobody could take the life of God-in-flesh and expect him to stay dead. We're not surprised because Jesus raised Lazarus, and we know he had the power of life and death. With all the power in the world,

Jesus says, I'm the One whose flesh will be eaten. After I wash the disciples' feet, I will lay down my life. This is my glory. This is John's Gospel. This is the good news John has to share.

And John bookends the story of God's self-revelation and self-sacrifice with the claim that we can be sons and daughters of God. How? By the grace of God and the daring faith of Jesus who gave himself for us, and now he calls us to daring faith as well. Daring faith is another way to describe obedience. Jesus was obedient in willingly giving his life. Obedience is not some kind of work that saves us. Obedience is being like Jesus. This obedient faith led Jesus to a cross. This obedient faith also leads us to a cross-shaped life.

We've read and heard people say that Jesus was crucified so we would not have to suffer the same things. The very heart of what Jesus said about laying down life for your friends is the heart of Christianity: having power and willingly giving it up for the sake of others. This does not mean purposeful suicide or getting ourselves killed by doing or saying dumb things, but it does mean we live in such a way that fear does not drive us. Instead, the relationship we have with a self-giving God does drive us.

So, how do we take in this irony of God doing a very "un-Godlike" thing? How do we take in the wonder of God's ultimate self-revelation at the cross? How do we participate in the life of the God who gives in such an un-Godlike way?

What does our life look like? Cross-shaped. The cross shapes our lives; by the mystery and wonder of a God who loves us so much that he dies for us willingly. If we believe, we have the right to be children of God who grow in this new reality to be servants, to take on a new identity of light, life, and truth. When we accept the analogies into our actual lived experience, Jesus's analogy of being the True Vine calls us to remain in him, including in the cross.

For more about how to live cross-shaped lives, we recommend a resource that was foundational for us. Our friend C. Leonard Allen has spoken much about cruciformity in his book, *The Cruciform Church*. Leonard and our friend John Barton have spoken recently about cruciformed lives, and we think you can find audio of those presentations through Pepperdine University or Abilene Christian University lectureship recordings online.

Nicodemus Must Appear Again

We left Nicodemus in John 3 in the twilight, between darkness and light. Jesus's words to him at night had left him scratching his head, but he doesn't walk away and reject Jesus. He's muttering, "How can this be?"

I need to meet Nicodemus again. He's so perplexed. I want to know how he works this out. Thankfully, John gives us two more views of Nicodemus growing in daring faith as a result of that first chat with Jesus.

The next time we find Nicodemus (7:45–52) he is with his fellow-Pharisees and the chief priests. The lynch mob gunning for Jesus is stirring against the growing wave of support for the prophet from Nazareth. The Jews want their guards to seize Jesus, but they are awestruck and tell the religious leaders, "We've never heard a man talk this way." The ruling council explain this behavior by saying, "There is a curse on these people." Do they think Jesus or someone has cursed the crowds, and that's why they are following him?

This is where Nicodemus comes back into John's story a second time. To his fellow-Jewish religious leaders, he promotes a common sense notion of justice that we're familiar with: a person is innocent until proven guilty. We can't railroad him without a trial. So Nicodemus stands for justice, though he stops short of claiming Jesus is the Messiah. He knows well that faithing Jesus in front of the ruling council will land him outside the Temple courts, stripping him of all social standing, religious influence, and economic abundance.

Do we do the basic thing of standing up for Jesus, with our co-workers, neighbors, family, and friends and saying to them, "Have you ever given Jesus a fair look?" I think that's what Nicodemus in the twilight was doing. He takes a step out of the darkness and toward the light of Jesus by standing for truth.

In John 19, we get a third and last picture of Nicodemus. Nicodemus leaves Jesus scratching his head in the darkness in John 3, and in John 7 he's in the twilight, still a secret admirer of Jesus, standing up for a principle but without the singularly risky proposition of standing up for Jesus. Now in John 19, Jesus has been crucified. A man named Joseph of Arimathea offers to bury Jesus in his own tomb. Jesus isn't laid in a "borrowed tomb" as some have said. I can't imagine that Joseph ever expects it will be a short-term interment. He is giving Jesus this property; nothing borrowed here.

Joseph comes to take Jesus's body down from the cross, and his friend, Nicodemus, tags along to help. With good reason. It will take two men to lug seventy-five pounds of aloes and myrrh to give Jesus a proper Jewish burial. The text says Joseph is a disciple, but secretly, for fear of the Jews. Seems Joseph and Nicodemus are a two-man Secret Jesus Burial Society. But what they are doing can hardly be kept secret.

Joseph's tomb is in a new section of the garden near Golgotha outside the city of Jerusalem. This doesn't seem like a private, secret act by Nicodemus and Joseph. Are Joseph and Nicodemus, though they are afraid, stepping out of the darkness? Giving Jesus a proper burial, touching an unclean dead body at Passover time, risking everything for the one they believe to be the Messiah is daring faith.

Joseph and Nicodemus must be getting closely acquainted with the dead body of Jesus, the holes in his hands, and his feet. They wrap him with aloes and myrrh, a mummy as Lazarus had been, and place him in Joseph's tomb.

Jesus is crucified on a Friday afternoon. The men would place Jesus in the tomb the same day. Jesus's body remains in the tomb on the Sabbath or Saturday. Then on Sunday morning, Mary Magdalene discovers the empty tomb. The synoptic Gospels mention other women present when they discover the empty tomb, but they don't mention Nicodemus helping Joseph, and they also differ on whether the Passover that year was on Friday or Saturday, but we generally say Jesus rose on the "third day."

When Jesus rises from the dead and appears to his disciples and tells them, "Put your hands right here in the holes," I believe Nicodemus is there. We don't know it from the text that Nicodemus is there after resurrection, but I bet he is. Nicodemus took a step out of the darkness, into twilight, now into the light. He moves out from undercover Christ-follower and takes a step into the light. And when Jesus rises from the dead, Nicodemus knows he had taken those risky steps of daring faith in the right direction, toward the Messiah.

—*Greg*

TRUTH & DARE

DARE ELEVEN

Read John 18–20

1. What stands out to you about how Christ is in control throughout his passion?

2. What do you dislike and like about the story of the crucifixion of Jesus in John?

3. What specific action or inaction does God seem to want from you, from others, from the church?

4. What actions, words, attitudes of yours are not obedient to this teaching you've read today?

5. Who is a person with whom God wants you to share what you've learned from the Gospel of John this week?

6. Pray for the courage to live a cruciformed, cross-shaped life, and ask God to show you what that means in your life.

DARE TWELVE:
Coming Back

"Believing in him is not the same as believing things about him such as that he was born of a virgin and raised Lazarus from the dead. Instead, it is a matter of giving our hearts to him, of come hell or high water putting our money on him, the way a child believes in a mother or a father, the way a mother or a father believes in a child."
—Frederick Buechner

THE BOOK OF JOHN ENDS WITH JESUS PICKING somebody up after he's really crashed. And, of course, it's the incredibly daring Peter. Peter, who dares to follow closely with Jesus, has an enormous spiritual failure at the end of the book. It's a quiet ending to the Gospel; Jesus powerfully, gently puts Peter back together after a total spiritual disintegration. And he shows us how to pick somebody up after they've really crashed. It's a great way for John's book to end. Because anybody who dares to live the life of Jesus at some point along the way is going to have a crash.

Sometime, somewhere in your life, someone you care about is going to crash. It may even be you. What happens after that is partly going to determine whether or not that person is going to get back up and follow Jesus. And whether or not we are able to do that for one another is going to have a lot to say about what the body of Christ is going to look like in the future. Only those who dare to follow, fail. It's like riding a bike or a skateboard. You won't be able to ride unless you are willing to take a tumble now and then. People are going to fall. And it's up to the rest of us to take that person who crashed and help them to get up and ride again. In this second quieter ending of John, Jesus gives us the model for putting people back together after they have experienced spiritual failure.

The second ending reminds us of a symphony that ends with a crash of symbols and then adds something quiet at the end. If you've attended many performances of classical music, you may have noticed this: many really good symphonies never get performed. The ones that seldom get performed are ones that end softly. They are really good classical pieces, but there's one simple reason these don't get performed in concert halls. Nobody knows when to clap. The audience doesn't know when it's over. It just sort of dissolves like the cough drop in your mouth. The symphonies you most often hear in concert halls across the United States end in a big loud note, and we all know it's over and time to applaud, and then leave.

John's ending is interesting because he ends his symphony at 20:30–31, with this incredible crescendo,

> Jesus performed many other signs in the presence of his disciples, which are not recorded in this book. But these are written that you may believe that Jesus is the Messiah,

> the Son of God, and that by believing you may have life
> in his name.

But John doesn't stop there. You hear the symbol clash and the final dramatic note, and that should be the end. There's a pause. Then he adds a little coda at the end, and it's an incredible gift to the Christian faith and how we see our relationship to Jesus, told through the experience of Peter, who is featured in John much less than in the other Gospels. But this story to John is worth the value of all the others. It's a compelling and powerful story of the restoration of a friend who has wronged Jesus.

John in this little coda has one more story to tell after the crescendo. There are four episodes of Jesus appearing to his followers after the resurrection.

First, Jesus appears to Mary Magdalene near the tomb.

We know four important things about Mary Magdalene (John 20:1–18; Luke 8:1–3): first, she had a terrible demon possession with seven evil spirits tormenting her. Second, Jesus healed her of that possession. Third, Mary Magdalene not only followed Jesus but joined a group of women in supporting Jesus in his ministry and travel logistics. Fourth, she is the top-rated witness to the empty tomb, and John singles her out as having been there alone to see Jesus first among all the disciples. All four Gospels include Mary Magdalene as one of the first witnesses of the empty tomb. John prioritizes this powerful moment with Jesus and Mary Magdalene in his telling of the risen Messiah.

> Early on the first day of the week, while it was still dark,
> Mary Magdalene went to the tomb and saw that the stone

had been removed from the entrance. So she came running to Simon Peter and the other disciple, the one Jesus loved, and said, "They have taken the Lord out of the tomb, and we don't know where they have put him!"

So Peter and the other disciple started for the tomb. Both were running, but the other disciple outran Peter and reached the tomb first. He bent over and looked in at the strips of linen lying there but did not go in. Then Simon Peter came along behind him and went straight into the tomb. He saw the strips of linen lying there, as well as the cloth that had been wrapped around Jesus' head. The cloth was still lying in its place, separate from the linen. Finally the other disciple, who had reached the tomb first, also went inside. He saw and believed. (They still did not understand from Scripture that Jesus had to rise from the dead.) Then the disciples went back to where they were staying.

Now Mary stood outside the tomb crying. As she wept, she bent over to look into the tomb and saw two angels in white, seated where Jesus' body had been, one at the head and the other at the foot.

They asked her, "Woman, why are you crying?"

"They have taken my Lord away," she said, "and I don't know where they have put him." At this, she turned around and saw Jesus standing there, but she did not realize that it was Jesus.

He asked her, "Woman, why are you crying? Who is it you are looking for?"

> Thinking he was the gardener, she said, "Sir, if you
> have carried him away, tell me where you have put him,
> and I will get him."
>
> Jesus said to her, "Mary."
>
> She turned toward him and cried out in Aramaic,
> "Rabboni!" (which means "Teacher").
>
> Jesus said, "Do not hold on to me, for I have not yet
> ascended to the Father. Go instead to my brothers and
> tell them, 'I am ascending to my Father and your Father,
> to my God and your God.'"
>
> Mary Magdalene went to the disciples with the news:
> "I have seen the Lord!" And she told them that he had
> said these things to her. (20:1–18)

After Jesus appears to Mary Magdalene, he appears to the apostles next. Not only does John put the apostles second in line of appearances by Jesus, but he also has less to say about this one, though what he does tell is potent.

> On the evening of that first day of the week, when the
> disciples were together, with the doors locked for fear of
> the Jewish leaders, Jesus came and stood among them
> and said, "Peace be with you!" After he said this, he
> showed them his hands and side. The disciples were over-
> joyed when they saw the Lord.
>
> Again Jesus said, "Peace be with you! As the Father
> has sent me, I am sending you." And with that he
> breathed on them and said, "Receive the Holy Spirit. If
> you forgive anyone's sins, their sins are forgiven; if you do
> not forgive them, they are not forgiven." (20:19–23)

In John's Gospel, Jesus appears a third time after the resurrection, and from how John tells it, this appearance is specifically for Thomas. Why does Jesus single out Thomas? Thomas had missed the earlier resurrection party for some reason. And maybe it was sour grapes, but after he'd missed seeing Jesus with the rest of the apostles, Thomas had been adamant that not only an appearance but also a physical exam would be required before he'd put his faith in Jesus!

Thomas says, "Unless I see the nail marks in his hands and put my finger where the nails were, and put my hand into his side, I will not believe" (20:25).

John graciously includes this story that rings down through two millennia in the ears of doubters, people like us who have not seen Jesus face to face. But we don't get to put our hands in Jesus's wounds. Yet, if you look closely, Jesus pronounces a blessing—through a comment to Thomas—on all future believers who do not see or touch but believe anyway.

"Because you have seen me, you have believed; blessed are those who have not seen and yet have believed" (20:29).

Those who have not seen and yet believed would be everybody John is writing to and every future reader. We haven't seen Jesus, but if we still believe, Jesus blesses us.

The last appearance of Jesus is the extra story after John's final crescendo. Because the ending is simple in its beauty, we are resisting trying to add much noise to it.

The final post-crescendo episode in the Gospel of John is a fishing story, but it's truly not about fish as much as it is about the restoration of Peter. The story begins with Peter saying he's going fishing. Some of the other disciples say, "We'll go with you." They fish all night but catch nothing. Then Jesus appears to them.

Early in the morning, Jesus stood on the shore, but the disciples did not realize that it was Jesus.

He called out to them, "Friends, haven't you any fish?"

"No," they answered.

He said, "Throw your net on the right side of the boat and you will find some." When they did, they were unable to haul the net in because of the large number of fish.

Then the disciple whom Jesus loved said to Peter, "It is the Lord!" As soon as Simon Peter heard him say, "It is the Lord," he wrapped his outer garment around him (for he had taken it off) and jumped into the water. The other disciples followed in the boat, towing the net full of fish, for they were not far from shore, about a hundred yards. When they landed, they saw a fire of burning coals there with fish on it, and some bread.

Jesus said to them, "Bring some of the fish you have just caught." So Simon Peter climbed back into the boat and dragged the net ashore. It was full of large fish, 153, but even with so many the net was not torn. Jesus said to them, "Come and have breakfast." None of the disciples dared ask him, "Who are you?" They knew it was the Lord. Jesus came, took the bread and gave it to them, and did the same with the fish. This was now the third time

Jesus appeared to his disciples after he was raised from the dead.

When they had finished eating, Jesus said to Simon Peter, "Simon son of John, do you love me more than these?"

"Yes, Lord," he said, "You know that I love you."

Jesus said, "Feed my lambs."

Again Jesus said, "Simon son of John, do you love me?"

He answered, "Yes, Lord, you know that I love you."

Jesus said, "Take care of my sheep."

The third time he said to him, "Simon son of John, do you love me?"

Peter was hurt because Jesus asked him the third time, "Do you love me?" He said, "Lord, you know all things; you know that I love you."

Jesus said, "Feed my sheep. Very truly I tell you, when you were younger you dressed yourself and went where you wanted; but when you are old you will stretch out your hands, and someone else will dress you and lead you where you do not want to go." Jesus said this to indicate the kind of death by which Peter would glorify God. Then he said to him, "Follow me!" (21:4–19)

The build-up to this story is a heartbreaking spiritual failure. Peter denies that he even knows Jesus. Often when we say something out of line, a little off-color, biting against someone, our conscience bothers us, and we start backpedaling. Not Peter. He denies his friend, the one he called his Lord, not once but three times. His three-time denial of Jesus is nothing less than a total spiritual meltdown, and we should not be surprised. In fact, it strangely heartens us as disciples to know that Bible stories show this truth vividly over and over in the lives of men and women who fail, like we do.

Nobody experiences life as an unbroken string of spiritual successes. Spiritual failure happens in our own lives and in those we care about. The story of how Jesus puts Peter back together is one of John's most compelling tales. We authors have read this story many times, but the first time either of us thought much about it was when we heard a really fine scholar-preacher point out that different words for *love* are used here.

The way we began to read the passage as a result of this new insight was to view the conversation between Jesus and Peter as a sort of progression of Greek words for love. Some of you already know the different Greek words for love, and it seems that two of them are being played here in John's re-creation of a conversation that probably took place originally in Aramaic. We'll take what was likely an Aramaic conversation, re-created in Greek by the Holy Spirit through John more than fifty years later, and write everything in English except for those two Greek words.

"John, do you *agape* me?" *Agape* is a word everybody thinks is the profound, deep love of God that we share. It's unconditional. Then there is *philos*, which is a kind of friendship love. That's why we call Philadelphia "the city of brotherly love." We admire or like something about a person, and that is *philos* love.

So in response to Jesus's question, "Do you *agape* me?" Peter responds, "I *philos* you."

Jesus asks a second time, "Do you *agape* me?"

"I *philos* you."

Having received the same avoidance response from Peter more than once, Jesus seems to adjust the question by changing the word to reflect the wavelength Peter is on.

"Peter, do you *philos* me?"

"You know I *philos* you, Lord."

The way we've always taught this passage is this: Peter doesn't have the *agape* thing going, so Jesus downshifts his language, cuts his losses, takes the lowest common denominator, gets on Peter's level, and starts with the admirable *philos* kind of friendship love to restore Peter.

That's a very compelling way to read this story of Jesus and Peter at the end of John. We have just one problem with this reading. We have come to believe it's wrong. Not that the words are not there or accurate. But John uses word variety in other places, and we can't always read into them what we want. Sometimes when we hear people use the same word over and over, it grates on us, and we wish they'd spend some time with *Reader's Digest Word Power* to build their vocabulary. We grate on ourselves sometimes when we hear the same word coming out of our mouths over and over. John uses different words sometimes, but it doesn't always mean he's doing so for anything else but variety.

We believe something else is going on here entirely, that the key to reading this story is not the verbs in Greek but something else. What we think we have in this fascinating scene is a model for how Jesus puts people back together when they've had an enormous spiritual crash.

Now, that's something we could all use, for ourselves and others.

Could it be that Jesus asks Peter three times if he loves him, because Peter denied him three times? Jesus is going to put Peter back together as thoroughly as he has come apart.

We believe in one-point sermons, but there are three points here, so for those who preach, you've got three Sundays of material here.

First, Jesus starts with the most important question when you've had spiritual failure. Do you love me? Jesus understands when a life has been shattered and you are trying to put it back together, you have to get first things first. The question Peter needs to answer first is, Do you love Jesus? It can be a painful question to ask someone who is a longtime Christian, but it's one we often ask people who have had some spiritual failure. Do you love Jesus? Once you've been able to say yes to this question, all things are possible.

Come to Breakfast!

My wife's maternal grandmother, until she died a centenarian, would call the family gathered at her house for holidays with a two-syllable word she would holler like no one else. In an East Texas drawl, she'd sing out, "Break . . ." in a low voice and ". . . fast" in a high-sustained voice. If ever there was a matriarch around whom everyone wanted to be, it was Ma. And when she said, "Break-fast!" we'd drop what we were doing and come to the table for farm-fresh sausage, bacon, biscuits, homemade jams, eggs, and strong coffee.

One of the best resource books today for Spiritual Walk of Life 101 is *Living God's Love* by our friends Earl Lavender and Gary Holloway. At the end of one of the chapters the authors ask their readers to draw a picture of God.

In response to their invitation to draw a picture of our view of God, I drew this scene from 21:1–14 with the caption, "Come to breakfast."

I drew the lake, the sunrise, the fire. I sketched the old logs Jesus may have dragged up for them to sit on. The resurrected Lord made breakfast for his disciples. It's hard to imagine eating fish for breakfast, but really anytime is time to eat fresh-from-the-lake, grilled fish. This lakeside scene draws me to the Father of Light and Love, the Holy Spirit Fire, and the Risen Son of Man. Friendship with God. Come to breakfast.

Later Jesus will take Peter aside and ask what his love is made of. Do you love me, Peter? Feed my sheep. The calling, the empty promises to stay with Jesus till death, the denial, the shame of Peter have devastated the fisherman, and now Jesus is holding up Peter's head and saying, "Come to breakfast and eat with me." The Kingdom is new, and Peter will be an instrument of peace in God's hands. These broken men are breaking bread together with God, the bread of life.

> And Jesus is there saying to his disciples, Come to breakfast that I'm providing. I don't call you disciples anymore. I call you friends. Come to breakfast, my friends, and taste what is good.
>
> Break-FAST!
>
> *—Greg*

Despite enormous failure, Peter loves Jesus. Jesus not only asks Peter, "Do you love me?" but he also commands Peter three times, "Care for my sheep." Peter may be inclined to think that, because of his failure, he has no part in the future Kingdom of God. After all, he's gone fishing again. Does he believe his apostleship has been revoked?

Peter later becomes one of the key leaders of the church, but not necessarily in spite of what he did. He may have been more useful to God's purposes precisely *because* he failed, and he knew it. Why? Because before his failures Peter seems pretty arrogant. He's glib. He's none of those things anymore.

We authors have been on both sides of preparing students for ministry and helping hire them to minister in churches. When a church leadership or search team asks, "Will this guy be a good minister?" we often say something like this: "He'll be a great minister, but he hasn't failed at anything yet. You really don't know a person until failure comes. Then true colors show. After failure, he may truly become a great minister."

Here, after Peter has failed, Jesus comes back around each time and says, "Feed my sheep." Far from being disqualified from ministry, now you're useful to me. "Care for my lambs." When we're trying to recover or help somebody else recover from a spiritual meltdown, one of the things that has to happen is that the failed person has to get their eyes off themselves and start to look at somebody else.

The world really doesn't revolve around our spiritual success or failure. Jesus first asks, "Peter, do you love me?" Then he says, "Feed my sheep." Then at the end Jesus says something chilling to Peter. In effect, Jesus tells him that things are never going to be the same as they were before. You know, Peter, we had those times when we were walking and talking around the lake and life was good, right? Things have changed. You're headed to a different place. Jesus gives a cryptic description of Peter's death. We have this tendency in our faith to want to be nostalgic, but there can be no faith for yesterday. There's only a faith for today. Peter's faith is scarred in ways that it wasn't before, but scars are not the opposite of faith.

Scars are part of faith. The relationships we've had with our parents have evolved through the years. You go through a time when you're a child and you think your parents are perfect. Then as a teenager you discover that they are far from perfect but average, as it seems with all people we live with. Mark Twain said, "When I was a boy of fourteen, my father was so ignorant I could hardly stand to have the old man around. But when I got to be twenty-one, I was astonished at how much the old man had learned in seven years." You are at least trying more at age twenty-one, but you continue growing in a relationship that isn't based on your parents' perfection. You mature and realize this relationship must be built on mutual failure, forgiveness, and love.

Faith needs to mature that way too. Our failures and our scars in faith are part of maturity. It is absolutely useless to wish for the faith of yesterday. Daring faith is real today, scars and all. Jesus doesn't want Peter looking backwards. He wants Peter and us looking forward without denying our spiritual failures. Scars become the stuff of our faith for today and tomorrow.

Jesus does three beautiful things to put Peter back together after a spiritual failure. First, he goes back to the basics. Do you love me? Second, he tells him, in effect, get your eyes off yourself and look at other people. I still have ministry for you to do. Third, Jesus re-focuses him onto what lies ahead. We can't think about yesterday. We've got to think about today and tomorrow. Nostalgia is one of the great enemies of daring faith. One of the most serious obstacles for seeing what God is doing today is the fading memory of what God has done in the past. A friend of ours, Wade Hodges, says it like this: The greatest hindrance to your next spiritual experience is your last one.

Some of us want to freeze-frame our spirituality, hold it there forever, partly because we're lazy, partly because we're afraid of going deeper into the life of God, afraid of what he might ask us to do. Feed my sheep. You're going to die, Peter. We may be just as apprehensive about these things as Peter is. We're all going to die. What better way to die than in his service? For Peter, faith is about today and tomorrow, which will be glorious. Good thing John didn't end the Gospel with a big loud note at the end of chapter 20.

We're happy John added this little coda, because we've had spiritual failures like Peter, and so have you. Watching Jesus put Peter back together is enormously comforting. It's a great way to end a book. Not with a cymbal clash, but in a quiet moment by the lake.

> This is the disciple who testifies to these things and who wrote them down. We know that his testimony is true. Jesus did many other things as well. If every one of them were written down, I suppose that even the whole world would not have room for the books that would be written. (21:24–25)

So now we come to the end. The question comes to you as readers. What about your faith is daring? John has shown us that Jesus is worth following, worth getting kicked out of the synagogue for. Jesus Christ is worth losing your security for, because Jesus truly is the Messiah, the Christ, the anointed One, the One for whom we have been waiting. The question now comes back to you: Is the Messiah worth daring faith?

TRUTH & DARE

DARE TWELVE

Read John 21

1. What stands out to you about the story of how Jesus put Peter back together?

2. What do you dislike and like about the story of Jesus restoring Peter?

3. What specific action or inaction does God seem to want from you, from others, from the church?

4. What actions, words, attitudes of yours are not obedient to this teaching you've read today?

5. Who is a person with whom God wants you to share what you've learned from the Gospel of John this week?

6. Do you need to pray for restoration like Peter received from Jesus?

7. Do you love Jesus?

FURTHER READING
On the Book of John

Ashbrook, Tom. *Mansions of the Heart: Exploring the Seven Stages of Spiritual Growth*. San Francisco: Jossey-Bass, 2009.

Barclay, William. *The Gospel of John*. Louisville: Westminster John Knox Press, 2001.

Bauckham, Richard. *The Testimony of the Beloved Disciple: Narrative, History, and Theology in the Gospel of John*. Grand Rapids: Baker Academic, 2007.

Brown, Raymond E. *The Gospel According to John*, 2 vols. Anchor Bible Commentaries. New York: Doubleday, 1966–1970.

Brown, Raymond E. *A Retreat with John the Evangelist*. Cincinnati: St. Anthony Messenger Press, 1998.

Card, Michael. *John: The Gospel of Wisdom*. Downers Grove, IL: InterVarsity Press, 2014.

Carson, Donald A. *The Gospel According to John*. Pillar Commentary Series. Grand Rapids: Eerdmans, 1991.

Fleer, David and Dave Bland. *Preaching John's Gospel: The World It Imagines*. St. Louis: Chalice Press, 2008.

Gordon, S. D. (Samuel Dickey). *Quiet Talks on John's Gospel*. Public Domain Books, 1915. Kindle Edition.

Just, Felix, S.J. "The Johannine Literature Web." http://catholic-resources. org/John (accessed July1, 2013).

Kysar, Robert. *John: The Maverick Gospel*. 3rd ed. Louisville: Westminster John Knox Press, 2007.

Peterson, Eugene H. *The Jesus Way: A Conversation on the Ways Jesus Is the Way*. Grand Rapids: Eerdmans, 2007.

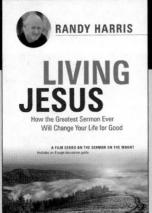
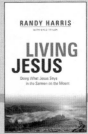

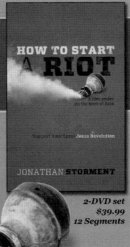